EDUCATION AND HIV/AIDS
A WINDOW OF HOPE

THE WORLD BANK

2 3 4 05 04

ISBN 0-8213-5117-6

Library of Congress Cataloging-in-Publication Data

World Bank:
    Education and HIV/AIDS: a window of hope / the World Bank.
       p.cm.
    Includes bibliographical references.
    ISBN 0-8213-5117-6
       1. AIDS (Disease)—Developing countries. 2. Education—Developing countries.
    3. Government aid to education. World Bank. I. Title.

RA643.86.D44 W67 2002
362.1'969792'0091724—dc21

2002022524

Contents

Boxes

Figures

Tables

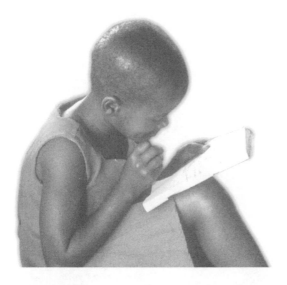

She **does not go to school any more.** For one thing, her small, rural school has been disintegrating under the impact of HIV/AIDS: teachers, already in short supply, have been dying, feeling too ill to teach, or moving to the city to seek medical care. For another, her grandparents—newly charged with the grandchildren after losing their own son and daughter-in-law to AIDS—have opted to spend their meager income on school fees for her two brothers, but not for her.

At age nine she does not have HIV/AIDS, but she is growing up without parents, without an education, and without the knowledge or resources to guide her choices in life. Her future partners or her future husband may well be HIV-positive. If so, she too, voiceless and powerless, will become infected. And if she lives long enough to have children, she will be unable to give them any better chance in life.

This paper is dedicated to her, and to giving all children like her a real chance for a better future.

Foreword

Human Immunodeficiency Virus/Acquired Immune Deficiency Syndrome (HIV/AIDS) continues its deadly course. The pandemic has already killed 25 million people, and 40 million more are currently infected. In the first year of the millennium, 5 million more people became infected. There is still no cure, and there is still no vaccine. Common thinking was that this disease was principally a public health challenge. That was wrong: HIV/AIDS is reversing decades of development gains, increasing poverty and undermining the very foundations of progress and security. The epidemic demands a response that confronts the disease in every sector, but education has a particularly important role to play.

The World Bank is a committed partner in the global effort to provide every child with access to a basic education. With more than 113 million children not in school in the poorest countries, this already presents a major challenge. However, HIV/AIDS makes this much greater in those countries where the education system was already struggling to grow, teachers are dying, or are too sick to teach. And every year more children are losing their parents and the support that allows them to go to school. Achieving Education for All in a world of AIDS presents an unprecedented challenge to the world's education community.

Responding to this challenge is essential for global development and for our collective mission to reduce poverty. However, it also offers a unique opportunity to help the next generation to weaken the deadly grip of HIV/AIDS. Even in the worst-affected countries most schoolchildren are not infected, and given the right opportunities and choices, they need not ever become infected with HIV. The schoolchildren of the world offer "a window of hope" into a better future, and their schools and teachers can help them to grow up with the knowledge, values and skills to seize that opportunity.

This paper lays out a strategic direction for the World Bank in responding to the impact of HIV/AIDS on education systems, and in helping develop an effective preventative response.

James D. Wolfensohn
President
The World Bank Group

Acknowledgments

This document was prepared by members of the World Bank's Education team led by Don Bundy and Manorama Gotur, with support from Lesley Drake and Celia Maier (Partnership for Child Development, U.K.), and under the direction of Ruth Kagia. Data on orphans were generously provided by Martha Ainsworth (Operations Evaluation Department) and Deon Filmer. Analyses relating to the Education and HIV/AIDS model were prepared by Nick Grassly, Kamal Desai, and Geoff Garnett (Partnership for Child Development and United Nations Programme on HIV/AIDS). We are grateful to Eric Swanson, Sulekha Patel, and Masako Hirago (Development Data Group) who collaborated in original analyses (figure 5-1) of the impact of HIV/AIDS on education indicators, and to Alain Mingat, Barbara Bruns, and the team who supported the analyses of the additional cost of achieving education for all in the presence of HIV/AIDS. Many other World Bank staff representing many sectors and networks have contributed to discussions of the issues considered here, and made important contributions to the reviewing process: Jayshree Balanchander, Jacques Baudouy, Rosemary Bellew, Regina Bendokat, Hans P. Binswanger, Eduard Bos, Jaap Bregman, Mariam Claeson, Shantayanan Devarajan, Michael Drabble, Sheila Dutta, Mourad Ezzine, Birger Fredriksen, Marito Garcia, Vincent Greaney, Salim Habayeb, Keith Hansen, Phil Hay, Robert Hecht, Emmanuel Jimenez, Bruce Jones, Elizabeth King, Yoshiko Koda, Karen Lashman, Jon Lauglo, Maureen Law, Elizabeth Lule, Mmantsetsa Marope, Angel Mattimore, Paud Murphy, Dzingai Mutumbuka, Mead Over, Robert Prouty, Omporn Regel, Michelle Riboud, Khama Rogo, Jamil Salmi, Lynne D. Sherburne-Benz, Ricardo Silveira, Jim Socknat, Shobhana Sosale, Steffi Stallmeister, Kalanidhi Subbarao, Amber Surrency, Mercy Tembon, Christopher Thomas, Alexandria Valerio, Lianquin Wang, Carolyn Winter, Hongyu Yang, Mary Eming Young, and Debrework Zewdie. We appreciated the inputs from our partner agencies, with special thanks to Helen Craig, Anna Maria Hoffmann, and Sheldon Shaeffer (UNESCO); Amaya Gillespie (UNICEF); Jack Jones and Inon Schenker (WHO); Anji Doka (UNDP); David Clarke (Department for International Development, United Kingdom); and Brad Strickland (U.S. Agency for International Development).

Acronyms and Abbreviations

AIDS	Acquired immune deficiency syndrome
CARICOM	Caribbean Economic Community
DfID	Department for International Development (United Kingdom)
Ed SIDA/AIDS	Education and HIV/AIDS
EFA	Education for All
FRESH	Focusing Resources on Effective School Health
HIPC	Heavily Indebted Poor Countries
HIV	Human immunodeficiency virus
MAP	Multicountry HIV/AIDS Program (for Africa)
MTT	Mobile Task Team on HIV/AIDS in Education (South Africa)
NGO	Nongovernmental organization
PRSP	Poverty Reduction Strategy Paper
STD	Sexually transmitted disease
U.N.	United Nations
UNAIDS	United Nations Programme on HIV/AIDS
UNESCO	United Nations Educational, Scientific, and Cultural Organization
UNICEF	United Nations Children's Fund
WHO	World Health Organization

Executive Summary

AIDS is turning back the clock on development. In too many countries the gains in life expectancy won are being wiped out. In too many countries more teachers are dying each week than can be trained. We will mainstream AIDS in *all* World Bank work.

James D. Wolfensohn, president of the World Bank,
address to the United Nations Security Council, January 2000

The central message of this paper is that the education of children and youth merits the highest priority in a world afflicted by HIV/AIDS. This is because a good basic education ranks among the most effective—and cost-effective—means of HIV prevention. It also merits priority because the very education system that supplies a nation's future is being gravely threatened by the epidemic, particularly in areas of high or rising HIV prevalence. Thus countries face an urgent need to strengthen their education systems, which offer a window of hope unlike any other for escaping the grip of HIV/AIDS. Vigorous pursuit of Education for All (EFA) goals is imperative, along with education aimed at HIV prevention.

AIDS destroys

The scale of the AIDS epidemic is enormous. By the end of 2001, over 40 million people were living with HIV/AIDS (UNAIDS 2001), nearly 25 million people had died of AIDS, and more than 15.6 million children under the age of 15 had lost their mother or both parents (U.S. Census Bureau 2000 estimates). As well as the human tragedy, the epidemic has a profound impact on growth and poverty: the United Nations Programme on HIV/AIDS (UNAIDS) estimates a loss of more than 20 percent of gross domestic product in the worst-affected countries by 2020.

The epidemic's grip on Africa has been by far the deadliest, but no part of the world is immune. The epidemic is on the upswing globally, spreading fastest in Eastern Europe, but also rising in the Caribbean. Data from Asia warn against complacency: national prevalence rates are currently low, but in some countries are similar to those in West Africa that are now recognized to be at the beginning of an epidemic, while India is second only to South Africa in the number of people currently infected (UNAIDS 2001).

Most devastating and far-reaching, perhaps, is the epidemic's impact on education systems. HIV/AIDS is draining the supply of education, eroding its quality, weakening demand and access, drying up countries' pools of skilled workers, and increasing the sector's costs. The full scope of the epidemic's impact on education becomes apparent when viewed in the context of the formidable challenges already confronting the sector. More than 113 million school-age children are out of school in developing countries, two-thirds of them girls. Of those who enter school, one out of four drops out before attaining literacy. At least 55 of the poorest countries seem unlikely to achieve EFA by 2015, and 31 of these countries are also among the 36 worst-affected by HIV/AIDS (see the appendix).

The time for business-as-usual is past. No country can afford not to act. The worst-affected countries need to arrest the epidemic's ravages and protect future generations, while low-prevalence countries need to recognize the speed with which complacency can lead to crisis and the tremendous opportunity for saving lives and financial resources through prevention.

Education matters

Countries need to accelerate their efforts toward achieving EFA goals, both because of the importance of education for a country's viability and because of the critical role it can play in preventing HIV/AIDS. Prioritizing education is crucial for the following reasons:

- Education is a major engine of economic and social development.

  ▸ *It drives a country's future.* Economic prosperity and the reduction of global poverty cannot be accomplished unless all children in all countries have access to, and can complete, a primary education of adequate quality.

  ▸ *It is pivotal to the achievement of several of the Millennium Development Goals,* adopted unanimously by 189 countries in September 2000. Education has powerful poverty-reducing synergies: one year of schooling for women lowers fertility by about 10 percent, while one or two years of schooling for mothers reduces child mortality by 15 percent.

- Education is a proven means to prevent HIV/AIDS.

  ▸ *It has been proven to provide protection against HIV infection.* A general basic education has an important preventive impact. It can equip children and youth to make healthy decisions concerning their own lives, bring about long-term healthy behaviors, and give people the opportunity for economic independence and hope.

  ▸ *It is among the most powerful tools for reducing girls' vulnerability.* Girls' education can go far in slowing and reversing the spread of HIV by contributing to female economic independence, delayed marriage, family planning, and work outside the home.

  ▸ *It offers a ready-made infrastructure for delivering HIV/AIDS prevention efforts* to large numbers of the uninfected population—schoolchildren—as well as youth, who in many countries are the age group most at risk.

  ▸ *It is highly cost-effective as a prevention mechanism,* because the school system brings together students, teachers, parents, and the community, and preventing AIDS through education avoids the major AIDS-related costs of health care and additional education supply.

Full speed ahead on EFA goals is vital. A general basic education—and not merely instruction on prevention—is among the strongest weapons against the HIV/AIDS epidemic. An urgent, strategic, and education-centered response by countries and their partners is of utmost importance.

HIV/AIDS has a direct impact on the education sector

A key objective of this paper is to expand awareness of the links between HIV/AIDS and education. Action is urgently needed, but will not be forthcoming or effective without an understanding of the nature of the epidemic's impact on education systems.

HIV/AIDS has an impact on the supply of education. While reliable data are limited, there is little doubt that the epidemic is seriously damaging the quantity and quality of education. Africa in particular appears to be experiencing sharp increases in mortality rates among teachers and administrators at all levels of education. Even where teachers are present, they may be sick and ineffective, or poorly qualified as schools either make do with whoever is available, or cut corners on training.

There is also an impact on the demand for education. For most countries, increases in the school-age population are expected. While the school-age population will be smaller than in the absence of AIDS, it will nonetheless continue to grow. Estimates by the U.S. Bureau of Census suggest that only 6 of the 26 countries worst affected by AIDS will show an actual reduction in the school-age population by 2015. In some countries, but not all, there is evidence of lower enrollment and higher dropout rates among orphans, perhaps particularly at the secondary and tertiary levels. Although the evidence is still unclear, the epidemic may reduce girls' access to education at all levels. Girls are highly vulnerable to contracting AIDS because of social, cultural, economic, and physiological reasons, and compared with boys are more often retained at home.

The World Bank has estimated the cost of achieving EFA by 2015 in low-income countries. As part of these analyses, a preliminary estimate has been made of the additional costs of achieving EFA that might be attributable to the impact of HIV/AIDS on education systems. HIV/AIDS is estimated to add between US$450 million and US$550 million per year (at U.S. dollar values for 2000, depending on other assumptions in the model) to the cost of achieving EFA in the 33 African countries studied. This implies that HIV/AIDS increases the total EFA external financing gap for these countries by about one-third.

HIV/AIDS increases education sector costs. On the supply side, budgets are having to accommodate higher teacher hiring and training costs to replace teachers who have died of AIDS, as well as the payment of full salaries to sick teachers who are absent and additional salary costs for substitute teachers. Zambia has estimated the epidemic's financial burden on the supply of teachers to amount to some US$25 million between 2000 and 2010, and Mozambique's estimate is about twice as much. Neither estimate includes demand-side costs, yet efforts to reach orphans and other vulnerable children are a rapidly growing new expenditure, especially in the worst-affected countries.

Country responses: Promising directions

A key objective of this paper is to offer useful input to decisionmakers faced with the responsibility for taking urgent action. The paper puts forward a set of promising directions that could make up such a response, informed by a review of country experience to date.

- *Pursuit of EFA goals.* Providing a basic education to children—while ensuring equal opportunities for girls—is among the most promising directions in responding to the AIDS epidemic. Supporting children, especially girls, to complete their secondary education is also a powerful tool in mitigating the circumstances that put youth at risk. Countries that have emphasized access as well as the quality of learning and sought innovative responses to long-standing constraints have seen the greatest advances.

- *Strategic planning.* Projecting the future needs of the education sector is an essential part of education planning. For the worst-affected countries there is an immediate need to protect and replace teachers; for all countries there is a longer-term need to ensure the stability and quality of supply.

- *School-based prevention programs.* Reproductive health programs begin in primary schools, with the aim of reaching students before they begin sexual activity, but must continue through all levels of education. The Focusing Resources on Effective School Health (FRESH) framework, which aims to focus resources on effective school health, was created by a partnership among the United Nations Educational, Scientific, and Cultural Organization; the World Health Organization; the United Nations Children's Fund; the World Bank; and others to provide a unified approach to school health.

- *Skills-based health education.* Information about sex and HIV is insufficient by itself to bring about low-risk behaviors, but must be linked with the development of interpersonal and other skills, such as critical and creative thinking, decisionmaking, and self-awareness, as well as with the development of the knowledge, attitudes, and values needed to make sound health-related decisions.

- *Peer education and focus on youth.* A powerful means to influence youth, peer education by respected students or other youth of the same age can help develop healthy behaviors and practices.

- *Support for orphans and out-of-school youth.* The burgeoning numbers of these disadvantaged children, and the lack of understanding of the constraints on their education, pose an enormous new challenge for which no tested solutions are available. The combination of little experience and weak data is potentially explosive and urgently needs attention. Innovation, cross-sectoral efforts, and information sharing to learn lessons quickly are essential to ensure that these children obtain a basic education.

- *Multimedia campaigns.* Countries can create support for and understanding of education sector HIV/AIDS prevention activities and promote community support by using communication strategies to reach large numbers of people through multiple channels: prime time television series, radio dramas, booklets, and other materials.

- *Partnership.* The success of the approaches described here depends heavily on strong collaboration and partnership across sectors, across stakeholders within a country (communities, families, government, the private sector, and nongovernmental organizations), and with and across international agencies.

Strategy for action

A broad strategic response rooted in education—and set within a national, multisectoral context—is essential for all countries. Responses to the HIV/AIDS epidemic have too often been piecemeal, small-scale, health-focused, and weakly integrated into related efforts. Strong political commitment is key to addressing such shortcomings. Particularly in low-prevalence countries, governments will need to recognize early on that complacency can be disastrous. The following four elements are central to an effective strategy:

- *Define objectives and targeted outcomes.* The starting point for an effective response is thus the affirmation of EFA goals and the express recognition that the education sector could be fortified to become a country's strongest weapon against HIV/AIDS, or, failing that, its worst victim, reversing decades of hard-won gains. Ensuring that children, especially girls, complete their secondary education is key to mitigating the circumstances that place youth at risk. Equally important is the need to establish key outcomes that can be monitored.
- *Expand the knowledge base.* A prerequisite for effective action is an adequate knowledge base to inform the development of immediate and long-term responses. Success will hinge on a strategy tailored to national circumstances. This step involves estimating the impact of HIV/AIDS on education supply and demand and on prospects for achieving EFA goals.
- *Identify appropriate actions, informed by a stocktaking process.* This paper urges countries to vigorously pursue national education goals, fully integrating an AIDS response into such efforts. It urges the development of a country-specific action program comprising measures drawn from a menu of promising approaches. Priorities of universal relevance are educating girls, delivering prevention messages to teachers and students at all levels, and ensuring that the supply of education is adequate in quality and quantity in relation to expected demand.
- *Find resources for financing actions.* Obtaining resources—whether from private investors, donors, or public sector allocation—entails competing for them. Countries will have to establish not only that need exists, but also that resources are being effectively used and producing results. Policy reforms aimed at improving

educational quality—and that help keep children in school—also serve to substantially lower countries' costs of achieving EFA and preventing HIV/AIDS.

The World Bank's role

The World Bank is a long-standing partner in the efforts of the poorest countries to educate their people, and is the largest external source of financing for education and for HIV/AIDS activities worldwide. The Bank is committed to supporting the world in an education-centered fight against AIDS, an objective that resonates strongly with its mission of poverty reduction. This fits squarely within the Bank's strategic framework, which emphasizes support for investment in people and progress toward the Millennium Development Goals.

The Bank's work in education is centered on two priorities. The first is EFA, which includes the objectives of universal primary education and gender equity in schooling. Second, the Bank's strategy for education recognizes that EFA is a first step along the continuum of lifelong learning to provide education for the knowledge economy, which is crucial to the development of skills and competencies that will strengthen national competitiveness in the global arena.

An urgent challenge is to integrate HIV/AIDS issues into the Bank's dual-focused support, as has most recently voiced by the Group of Eight Task Force on Education, established in 2001 to accelerate progress on EFA. For the Bank, this directive implies helping countries to pursue overall education goals more vigorously while factoring in the epidemic's impact, and to ensure adequate education aimed specifically at HIV/AIDS prevention. Countries drive this process by preparing nationally owned development strategies, articulated in Poverty Reduction Strategy Papers.

The broad principles that underlie all Bank support for education are as follows:

- *Scaling up successful approaches.* The Bank is working with partners to support countries throughout Africa in assessing the impact of HIV/AIDS on their education systems and planning an appropriate response using the Education and HIV/AIDS (Ed-SIDA/AIDS) approach, and to implement skills-based school health programs based on the FRESH framework.
- *Mobilizing resources.* The Bank is reinforcing political commitment for EFA, both as an end in itself and as an important weapon in fighting AIDS. There is a need to increase both the overall level of external support and the share of resources allocated to education.
  - ▶ The Bank is currently financing 143 education projects implemented in 78 countries, reflecting investments of US$9.7 billion. During the last five years,

new commitments for girls' education projects have averaged nearly 60 percent of total primary and secondary education lending. The Bank supports countries in modifying existing projects and in ensuring that new EFA and girls' education projects include a specific response to HIV/AIDS wherever relevant. All social sector projects may support education, and there is a specific aim to increase support for orphans and other vulnerable children.

▶ Debt relief under the Heavily Indebted Poor Countries Initiative is a landmark effort, carried out jointly with the International Monetary Fund, to mobilize global resources for some of the world's poorest countries. A total of US$36 billion in debt savings has been committed to 24 countries, where social spending is now projected to increase by some US$2.2 billion per year. Early indications are that some 40 percent of these extra resources will be directed to education and 25 percent to health.

▶ The multisectoral Multicountry HIV/AIDS Program for Africa has committed US$462.5 million to 12 countries, and a similar initiative has made US$53.5 million available to Caribbean countries. A multisectoral response is central to the strategy of these projects, and in the second phase of this approach, another US$500 million is being made available and the role of the education sector is being given specific emphasis.

■ *Generating and sharing knowledge.* The Bank is helping countries to draw on worldwide and regional best practice and to undertake analytical work to ensure sound approaches and effective use of resources, and is evaluating the impact of education system approaches across several countries. Expanding and consolidating Web-based "gateways" is another priority. The Bank is also working with partners to develop a sourcebook that brings together best practice on school-based prevention methods. Urgent priorities include assessing the impact of education responses to the AIDS epidemic and finding solutions to the challenges orphans and other vulnerable children face.

■ *Building capacity.* Bank support covers three important areas in relation to capacity building. First, the Bank helps ministries of education make the case—to national leaders, finance ministers, and the public—for an increase, not only in the share of resources for education, but in the overall level of support, commensurate with the importance of education. Second, the Bank seeks to expand its work with partners to provide training in the use of education planning tools such as the Ed-SIDA/AIDS model. Third, the Bank provides support for building education sector capacity to collect data and analyze education statistics.

■ *Working with strategic partners.* The Bank is a founding member of UNAIDS and a member of the United Nations Interagency Working Group on schools and education, a partnership that facilitates countries' development of strategic plans for HIV/AIDS prevention and impact management in education systems. The development and implementation of the FRESH framework and the Ed-

SIDA/AIDS model are examples of the importance of partnerships in the fight against AIDS. On EFA, the Bank is taking the lead in working with various partners to analyze the policy and resource gaps for meeting the goals and for assessing the impact of HIV/AIDS on the cost of achieving EFA.

- *Promoting innovation.* The Bank recognizes the need for innovative and flexible responses, in particular, for the worst-affected countries and the most vulnerable groups, such as orphans and youth.

HIV/AIDS is unequivocally the most devastating disease we have ever faced, and it will get worse before it gets better.

Dr. Peter Piot, executive director of UNAIDS, November 2001

1

HIV/AIDS and Why
Education Matters

Where we are today

The statistics are now familiar, but still staggering. Globally, 25 million people have died from AIDS. About 40 million people are estimated to be living with HIV or AIDS—a figure that is more than 50 percent above that projected in 1991 by the World Health Organization (WHO). While Sub-Saharan Africa accounts for nearly 70 percent of this total, all regions are affected (figure 1-1). AIDS orphans (defined as those who have lost either their mother or both parents) and other vulnerable children number some 15.6 million worldwide (U.S. Census Bureau cited in Hunter and Williamson 2000). The infection continues to spread rapidly: in 2001 alone, about 5 million people became newly infected (UNAIDS 2001).

Figure 1-1. Estimated number of adults and children living with HIV/AIDS, end of 2001

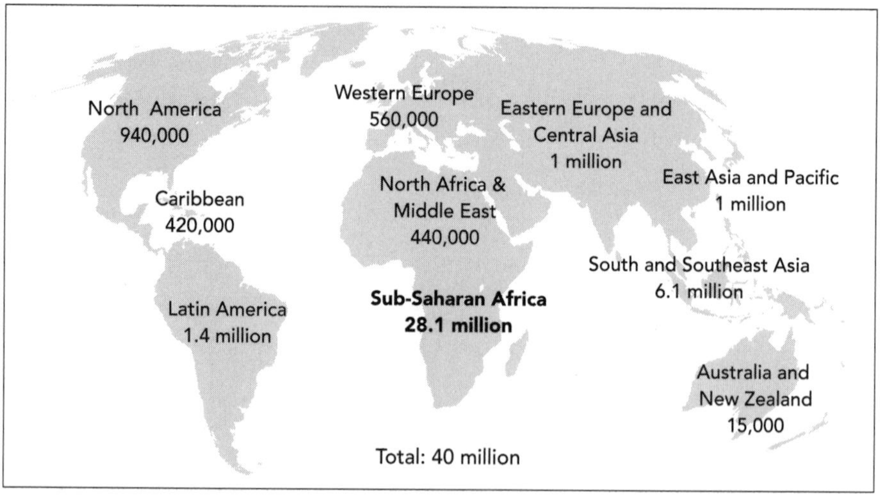

North America
940,000

Western Europe
560,000

Eastern Europe and
Central Asia
1 million

East Asia and Pacific
1 million

Caribbean
420,000

North Africa &
Middle East
440,000

South and Southeast Asia
6.1 million

Latin America
1.4 million

**Sub-Saharan Africa
28.1 million**

Australia and
New Zealand
15,000

Total: 40 million

Source: UNAIDS 2001.

Some 45 countries with HIV prevalence rates above 2 percent of the population are believed to be the worst affected by the HIV/AIDS crisis. Of these countries, 36 are in Africa, 7 with prevalence rates around 20 percent or higher. India deserves special mention: it is estimated to have a relatively low prevalence rate, but the highest number of AIDS deaths (1999) and the second highest number of people living with the infection (end of 1999). In many developing countries, especially in Sub-Saharan Africa, HIV/AIDS has spread from high-risk groups to the general population, and in many countries 60 percent of all new HIV infections occur among people aged 15 to 24.

The epidemic's grip on Africa has been by far the deadliest, but no part of the world is immune. Sub-Saharan Africa remains the epidemic's epicenter: average life expectancy is now 47 years, compared with an estimated 62 without AIDS (World Bank 2000b), and prevalence rates are the world's highest—more than 10 percent in 16 countries, and as high as 44 percent among some groups, for example, pregnant women in urban Botswana. Globally, the epidemic is on the upswing, spreading the fastest in Eastern Europe: new infections in the Russian Federation appear to be almost doubling annually since 1998. Data from Asia also warn against complacency. While national prevalence rates are low, they mask localized epidemics. Infection rates in Cambodia, Myanmar, and Thailand are in the 2 to 4 percent range, similar to those in many West African countries, while India is second only to South Africa in the number of people currently infected (UNAIDS 2001).

How we got here

Reversing the crisis is critically dependent on understanding its origins. While a detailed discussion of this topic is beyond the scope of this paper, key determining factors with high relevance for the education sector, particularly in Africa, include the following:

- The lack of information on how the infection can be contracted or prevented
- The powerlessness of women and young girls in many societies, resulting from a lack of education, economic independence, and legal rights
- The extended family networks that leave girl orphans especially vulnerable
- The wide prevalence, in some regions, of commercial sex, which people (including children) turn to for survival as a result of economic and political conditions, often exacerbated by sex tourism
- The sharing of needles among intravenous drug users
- The cultural and religious conservatism that constrains open discussion and information provisions about sexual matters in general, and about AIDS in particular, given its associated stigma
- The denial of the problem throughout the early years of the epidemic, including at national political levels, and the lack of political commitment, national prevention strategies, and coordinated response, all resulting in inaction and entrenchment of the disease.

Why education matters

An educated population and work force are fundamental to national health. Combined with sound macroeconomic policies, education is generally a key factor in promoting social well-being and poverty reduction, because it directly affects national productivity, which in turn determines living standards and a country's ability to compete in the global economy. To participate in knowledge-driven development, countries need to build their human capital. Moreover, global poverty cannot be reduced unless all children in all countries have access to, and can complete, a primary education of adequate quality.

Much of the macro- and microeconomic literature emphasizes the role of education in economic growth (Krueger and Mikael 2000). Accumulated research since the beginning of the 20th century provides robust evidence of a substantial social and private payoff to investment in education. The evidence points to a positive association between economic growth and change in education: growth increases with more education, and declines with less. No country has achieved economic growth without first assuring the education of its population. We can predict, with reasonable confidence, that for countries where

HIV/AIDS has significantly reduced average years of schooling or enrollment rates, the impact on education alone will dramatically constrain economic growth.

Investment in education is vital, because it promotes achievement of six of the eight Millennium Development Goals (box 1-1): reducing poverty, achieving universal primary education, improving gender equality, reducing infant and child mortality, improving maternal health, and lowering the prevalence of HIV/AIDS. Substantial evidence shows that education profoundly affects young people's reproductive lives. Better educated women are more likely, in comparison with their peers, to delay marriage and childbearing, have fewer children and healthier babies, enjoy better earning potential, have stronger decisionmaking and negotiation skills as well as higher self-esteem, and avoid commercial sex. Studies documenting the benefits of female education include reduced infant and maternal mortality, enhanced family health and welfare, and increased economic productivity (Odaga and Heneveld 1995). An analysis of data from 100 countries also found that an additional year of female education reduces the total fertility rate by 0.23 births (World Bank 2001a).

Box 1-1. The Millennium Development Goals

These goals were endorsed by 189 countries at the September 2000 United Nations Millennium General Assembly in New York.

1. Eradicate extreme poverty and hunger.
2. **Achieve universal primary education.**
3. **Promote gender equality and empower women.**
4. Reduce child mortality.
5. Improve maternal health.
6. Combat HIV/AIDS, malaria, and other diseases.
7. Ensure environmental sustainability.
8. Develop a global partnership for development.

Note: Education for All goals are shown in bold.

For boys and girls, education has been proven to provide protection against HIV infection (World Bank 1999). A basic education has a general preventive impact: it can inform children and youth and equip them to make decisions concerning their own lives, bring about long-term behavioral change, and give them the opportunity for economic independence—all fundamental to prevention, and therefore to hope (box 1-2). In addition, instruction focused on HIV/AIDS prevention is crucial to closing persistent fundamental gaps in knowledge: the latest report by the United Nations Programme on HIV/AIDS (UNAIDS) shows that 20 years into the epidemic, millions of young people, even in badly affected countries, are ignorant or have misconceptions about the disease (UNAIDS 2000a).

Box 1-2. Education: Why a window of hope?

- Children 5 to 14 years old represent one window of opportunity because they are the least likely to be infected with HIV. Education before they reach the peak vulnerable years will protect them, and this protection will be reinforced by early training that promotes healthy life styles and avoidance of risky behaviors.
- Youth 15 to 24 years old represent a second window. This high-risk group, which accounts for some 60 percent of all new HIV infections in many countries, is also the one where ignorance remains dangerously high and where education efforts can yield maximum results.

The evidence that education itself protects against HIV is strong. Data for the late 1980s and early 1990s, when the HIV/AIDS pandemic was just emerging, mostly showed a positive correlation between level of education and rates of infection. This was perhaps because the higher socioeconomic status and greater mobility of better educated people enabled encounters with a greater number and range of sexual partners, but also because at that time education seldom included HIV/AIDS prevention or behavioral change programs, and the level of knowledge about the disease was generally low. However, once the ways to avoid infection became better known, educated people were more likely to adopt safer behavior (World Bank 1999), and later studies show a reversal in the trend, with better educated people having lower rates of infection, especially among younger people (Gregson, Waddell, and Chandiwana 2001; Kelly 2000a; Vandemoortele and Delamonica 2000). A study in Zambia, for example, found a marked decline in HIV prevalence rates in 15- to 19-year-old boys and girls with a medium to higher level education, but an increase among those with lower educational levels (Kelly 2000c).

Note that the impact of education on behavior is strongest among the young, which may reflect the relative effectiveness of ensuring that a child grows up to practice good health behaviors, versus efforts to achieve behavior change among adults with established risky behaviors. This may explain why some teachers, who are often the best educated people in a community, still practice behaviors that contribute to the epidemic. However, the view that teachers are particularly at risk of infection or that the prevalence of HIV is higher among teachers than among adults in general does not appear to be supported (or denied) by any available evidence.

Despite today's generally high levels of basic awareness about HIV/AIDS, knowledge gaps persist. Such gaps can be dangerous, for example, where infected men seek out uninitiated girls with the aim of curing themselves. In South Africa, a third of survey respondents believed that HIV-positive people would always show symptoms. In Kenya, AIDS orphans—often in denial—believed that their parents had died from witchcraft or a curse. Surveys of 15- to 19-year-olds (1994–98) showed varying levels of knowledge across 17 countries (figure 1-2), with greater knowledge in countries with a longer history of AIDS (UNAIDS 2000a). Girls were generally more poorly informed than boys. A survey of schoolchildren in Botswana showed some knowledge gaps; a common perception of teachers is that many students are in denial and unable to accept that staff and students are being infected (Kelly 2000a; data from the Ministry of Health, Botswana). Other gaps include African university students' belief that oral contraceptives prevent HIV infection and that the virus can pass through an undamaged condom. Only 45 percent of surveyed students considered themselves at risk, manifesting "denial, fatalism, and an air of invulnerability" (Kelly 2001).

Figure 1-2. The information gap: Percentage of boys and girls aged 15 to 19 who did not know any way to protect themselves against HIV/AIDS, 1994–98

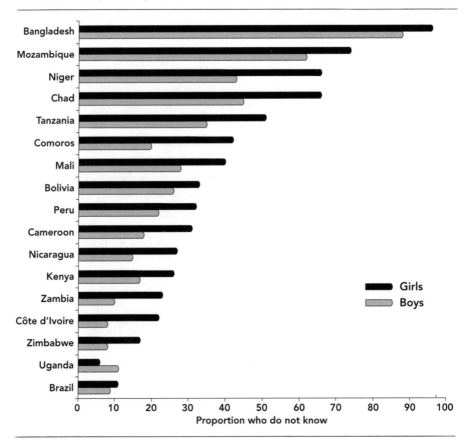

Source: Demographic and health surveys (1994–98); Macro International and United Nations Children's Fund data.

Education is among the most powerful tools for reducing the social and economic vulnerability that exposes women to a higher risk of HIV/AIDS than men (box 1-3). Girls' education can go far in slowing and reversing the spread of HIV by contributing to poverty reduction, gender equality, female empowerment, and awareness of human rights. It also has crucial implications for female economic independence, delayed marriage, family planning, and work outside the home.

Box 1-3. Education can protect women from HIV/AIDS

An analysis of demographic and household surveys from 32 countries since the early 1990s found that nearly half of all illiterate women lacked the basic knowledge to protect themselves against HIV/AIDS. Studies have shown that:

- Women with a postprimary education were three times more likely than uneducated women to know that HIV can be transmitted from mother to child.
- In Zimbabwe secondary education had a protective effect against HIV infection for women that extended at least into early adulthood (Gregson, Waddell, and Chandiwana 2001).
- In Zambia young women with a secondary education were less likely to be HIV-positive than those who had not received a secondary education (1995–97). During the 1990s the HIV infection rate fell by almost half among educated women, with little decline for women without any formal schooling (Vandemoortele and Delamonica 2000).
- In 17 countries in Africa and 4 in Latin America better-educated girls tended to delay having sex, and were more likely to require their partners to use condoms (UNAIDS 2000a).
- In Uganda, while infection rates among young women of all educational backgrounds fell, the decline was greatest for women with a secondary education (UNAIDS 2000a).

Countries' education sectors have a strong potential to make a difference in the fight against HIV/AIDS. They offer an organized and efficient way to reach large numbers of school-age youth—the groups either most at risk (secondary) or most receptive to efforts that seek to influence behavior (primary). Notwithstanding the ongoing need for considerable progress, many more children are in school today than ever before. The endorsement of the Education for All (EFA) initiative by 155 countries promises further expansion of the pool of children who can be reached (box 1-4). Secondary and tertiary education provides a means to reach a portion of the population that is important not in terms of numbers, but as a crucial resource of productive human capital for a country. As such, it affords a critical opportunity to scale up successful approaches, vital in view of the wide and rapid reach of the epidemic. In addition, the sector's reach extends to two other important groups: teachers and communities (including parents), who can play a crucial role in efforts to address the problem at its roots.

Box 1-4. EFA goals

EFA is a commitment taken on by the international community at the April 2000 World Education Forum in Senegal to achieve education for "every citizen in every society." Specifically, it commits the EFA partnership to ensure that by 2015 all children, especially girls, children in difficult circumstances, and those from ethnic minorities, have access to and complete free and compulsory education of good quality. In addition, it commits the partnership to eliminating gender disparities in primary and secondary education by 2005.

Education is highly cost-effective as a prevention mechanism. Countries where the epidemic is not yet at crisis proportions will, by preventing AIDS through education, avoid the health care and teacher supply–related costs that the worst-affected countries have to bear. The school system is also cost-effective in its ability to bring together students, teachers, parents, and the community, all of whom have to play a role in AIDS prevention.

Countries need to invest in the education sector not only for the crucial benefits it yields—overall and in an AIDS context—but also because no other sector may be more fundamentally threatened by the epidemic. In the worst-hit countries teachers are dying faster than they can be replaced, absenteeism is eroding the quality of education, and the problem of a rising orphan population—as high as 15 percent of all children—is demanding urgent national attention. The failure of education systems leads to a vicious cycle of deaths and decline in the sector, and the cycle is particularly vicious for girls. Already handicapped by less access to education than boys, girls may, as a result of the epidemic, be even less likely to attend school, either because they are themselves infected or because they are retained at home to care for patients. This pattern leaves them uneducated and unable to earn a living, protect themselves from infection, or break out of the social traps (such as abuse and early marriage) that expose them to increased risk of HIV infection.

Even without HIV/AIDS, the education sector faces major challenges. More than 113 million children aged 6 to 12 are out of school in developing countries, two-thirds of them girls. Progress toward internationally agreed-on goals set in 1990 under the EFA initiative and reconfirmed as part of the Millennium Development Goals in 2000 has been uneven and inadequate. A total of 55 of the poorest countries is estimated to be unable to achieve universal primary education by 2015, of which 31 are also among the 36 countries worst affected by HIV/AIDS (see the appendix). The goal of eliminating gender disparities in primary and secondary education by 2005 poses an even greater challenge, given the proximity of the target date as well as the greater likelihood of girls dropping out of school in the HIV/AIDS context. The regions at greatest risk of not meeting EFA goals are Africa and South Asia—with 80 percent of the out-of-school primary age population—and the Middle East and North Africa, with wide gender disparities.

An efficient education system will strengthen a country's response to HIV/AIDS. Recent work on 24 low-income countries shows the 9 countries on track to achieving universal primary enrollment by 2015 combine a relatively high education effort, reasonable unit costs, and a pupil-teacher ratio that ensures adequate educational quality (table 1-1). Low spending, high unit costs, and low quality mark 15 at-risk countries. Both groups have a significant share of countries with high HIV prevalence among young women. The greater educational efficiency of the on-track countries will enable a stronger response, as they bring prevention efforts to a higher proportion of children, allocate more resources (overall as well as per child), and exhibit higher educational quality in delivering prevention messages. Countries failing to achieve universal primary education because of below-average efficiency will also be less able to respond to the impact of HIV/AIDS. Thus those changes to the education system that can help low-income countries progress toward EFA will also help them respond better to HIV/AIDS.

Table 1-1. EFA progress in 24 low-income countries: Efficiency and potential protection against future risk of HIV/AIDS, 2000

Category	Allocation to the education sector (percentage of average per capita GDP)	Unit cost (multiple of average per capita GDP)	Mean gross enrollment ratio (percent)	Pupil-teacher ratio	Percentage of countries with > 5 percent HIV infections among young women
Countries not at risk on enrollment or 5th grade completion (9 countries)	4.2	10.4	> 90	39.7	44
Countries at risk on both enrollment and 5th grade completion (15 countries)	3.2	14.4	> 70	50.5	53

GDP: gross domestic product.

Source: World Bank estimates.

The tremendous potential of education and the crippling impact on education of the HIV/AIDS epidemic present both an enormous opportunity for countries that act and a grave danger for those that do not. The divergent paths will be most evident in Africa, where the predominance of youth in the population promises particularly rich rewards for an education-focused strategy, but dire consequences for a passive strategy that succumbs to the vicious cycle engendered by HIV/AIDS (figure 1-3).

Figure 1-3. HIV/AIDS and education: The consequences of inaction

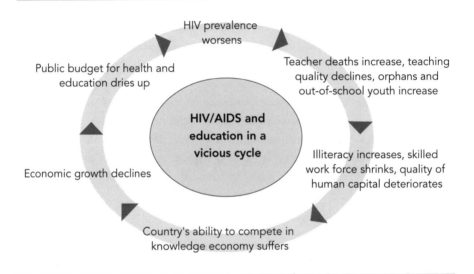

Source: Authors.

Full speed ahead on EFA goals is vital. In a message not yet widely understood, this paper argues that a general basic education—and not merely instruction on prevention—is among the strongest weapons against the HIV/AIDS epidemic, and that an urgent, strategic, and education-centered response by countries and their development partners is of utmost importance. The paper examines the epidemic's impact on the education sector, presents promising directions among country responses to date and a proposed strategy for action, and identifies the support under way and envisaged by the World Bank. The promising directions, which are based on early country experience, are presented with a view to sharing approaches that could provide timely, if not proven (with the benefit of evaluation), guidance to crisis or near-crisis countries that lack the luxury of time.

2

The Impact of HIV/AIDS
on Education

Supply and quality

HIV/AIDS has a pronounced adverse impact on both the supply and quality of education.

Teacher mortality

While many countries lack reliable data on AIDS-related deaths and HIV prevalence among teachers, available evidence points to an increased teacher mortality rate in the presence of HIV/AIDS (box 2-1). The death of one teacher deprives a whole class of children of education. An estimated 860,000 children in Sub-Saharan Africa lost teachers to AIDS in 1999 (Kelly 2000d). In southern Africa teachers are believed to have a higher HIV incidence than the general population, perhaps because of their relatively higher socioeconomic status, greater mobility, and postings away from home leads to more sexual contacts and therefore increased risk of infection. Even without assuming higher teacher risk, significant increases in teacher mortality are projected in seriously affected countries (figure 2-1). Death and illness are also affecting education sector administrators, finance and planning officials, inspectors, and managers in many African countries. These losses represent a loss of sector knowledge, with major negative consequences, including the transfer of in-service teachers to these positions. At least 12 percent of South Africa's administrative personnel are estimated to be HIV-positive (Coombe 2000a).

Box 2-1. HIV/AIDS and teacher supply: Evidence from Africa

- In the Central African Republic 85 percent of teachers who died between 1996 and 1998 were HIV-positive, and on average died 10 years before they were due to retire (UNAIDS 2000a).
- In Zambia 1,300 teachers died in the first 10 months of 1998, compared with 680 teachers in 1996 (Kelly 1999).
- In Kenya teacher deaths rose from 450 in 1995 to 1,500 in 1999 (reported by the Teaching Service Commission), while in one of Kenya's eight provinces 20 to 30 teachers die each month from AIDS (Gachuhi 1999).
- HIV-positive teachers are estimated at more than 30 percent in parts of Malawi and Uganda (Coombe 2000b), 20 percent in Zambia (Kelly 2000a), and 12 percent in South Africa (Coombe 2000a).

Figure 2-1. Average annual percentage of teachers who will die from AIDS, selected Sub-Saharan African countries, 2000–10

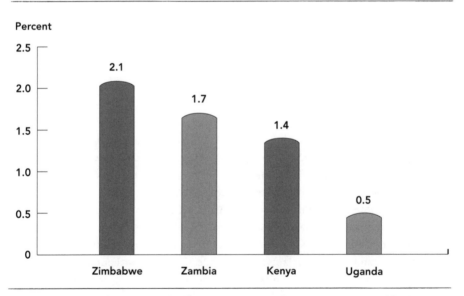

Note: Based on the assumption that teachers have the same infection rate as estimated for the general population.

Source: World Bank 2000b.

Absenteeism

HIV/AIDS increases teacher absenteeism. Less time for teaching and disruption of class schedules has meant reduced quality and quantity of education. Several factors contribute to absenteeism.

First, for infected teachers the illness itself causes increasing periods of absence from classes because of the progressive nature of the disease. According to a World Bank (1999) analysis, an infected teacher or education officer is likely to lose 6 months of professional time before developing full-blown AIDS, and a further 12 months after developing the disease. In Zambia, for example, a person is estimated to average 12 to 14 AIDS-related sickness episodes before the terminal illness (Kelly 2000a). A related problem is that to avoid or postpone the decline in remuneration that results from prolonged absence, infected teachers do not take formal sick leave. They are thus absent, but are not replaced with substitutes, as they remain formally in post earning a full salary. Substitution for these teachers requires a doubling of expenditures.

Second, teachers with sick families take time off to attend funerals or to care for sick or dying relatives. In several countries head teachers have reported problems with female teachers, in particular, arriving late or leaving work early. A recent survey in Botswana found that absenteeism among female teachers averaged 6.6 percent, compared with 3.3 percent for male teachers, and that funeral attendance was the second biggest factor (after illness) in AIDS-related absenteeism in schools, accounting for 7 to 12 percent of episodes of absenteeism. Funerals also result in several days of absence at a time.

Third, teacher absenteeism and nonperformance are also a result of the psychological effects of the epidemic. The trauma can be devastating, with repeated episodes of grief and mourning. Teachers may be deeply affected by having to care for sick relatives and losing friends and family to AIDS, with the added financial burden of medical and funeral expenses. In Zambia more than two-thirds of a survey sample of teachers with relatives who were ill with or had died of AIDS were unable or unwilling to talk about the problem with friends or family. Such isolation, as well as fear about their own HIV status, takes its toll on teachers and on their ability to teach (Kelly 2000a).

Rural drain

The supply of teachers in rural areas may be particularly badly affected. In Zambia posting teachers to rural areas has become increasingly difficult, with a resulting tendency for teachers to be concentrated in urban areas, partly because of AIDS-affected teachers' desire to be close to hospitals or clinics (Kelly 2000a).

Postbasic teachers

Since the onset of the HIV/AIDS epidemic, African universities are operating in a worsening socioeconomic environment. A recent study of seven African universities (in Benin, Ghana, Kenya, Namibia, South Africa, and Zambia) found an overwhelming atmosphere of ignorance, secrecy, denial, and fear of stigmatization and discrimination in relation to AIDS (Kelly 2001). Although information on staff and student mortality was vague and ambiguous, an increasing number of AIDS-related deaths has been reported. The University of Zambia reported an average of three deaths a month throughout the 1990s, while the University of Nairobi is currently experiencing four to six deaths a month. For university students, most of whom are in the age group most vulnerable to HIV infection, the real impact of infection will probably occur after graduation. The tragedy of HIV/AIDS is that primary, secondary, and tertiary students now affected are all potential teachers of the future. The impact of the disease thus ripples through generations to come.

Demand

The impact of the epidemic on demand for education is less clear. The school-age population will be smaller than in the absence of AIDS, but will nonetheless continue to grow. Reduced numbers of adults of childbearing age due to AIDS and lower fertility among surviving adults—not infection and mortality among children—have the largest impact on the numbers of children (box 2-2). The size of the school-age cohort is heavily influenced by fertility rates, and in many countries the relationship between HIV prevalence and the change in size of the 5- to 14-year-old age group appears to be weak. Estimates by the U.S. Census Bureau suggest that only 6 of the 26 countries worst affected by AIDS will show an actual reduction in the school-age population by 2015 (figure 2-2). In countries hardest hit by the epidemic, however, such as Zambia and Zimbabwe, the number of children of primary school age will be 20 percent lower by 2010 than pre-AIDS projections (UNAIDS 2000g). Other countries that have medium or declining levels of fertility can expect to experience significant declines in the school-age cohort as the epidemic progresses.

AIDS mortality does not have its primary effect on school-age children. The majority of children dying of AIDS are young children who have contracted the disease from mother-child transmission. An estimated 3.8 million children have been infected with HIV since the epidemic began, and more than two-thirds have died. UNAIDS estimates that in 1999, 570,000 children under the age of 15 became infected, and that 330,000 to 670,000 children under 14 have died of AIDS, the vast majority of them in Sub-Saharan Africa (UNAIDS 2000a). During this time, approximately four times as many adults (aged 15 to 49) died of AIDS.

Box 2-2. HIV infection rates among children and adolescents

- Throughout the world, HIV infection prevalence is lowest in the 5- to 14-year-old age group.
- Of children born with HIV because of vertical transmission from the mother, fewer than half survive to school age.
- Children born uninfected are unlikely to become infected until they reach adolescence and become sexually active.
- Prevalence among 15- to 19-year-old girls in Africa is often more than twice that of boys.
- Older children and young adolescents who contract HIV when they become sexually active are most likely to die in their 20s or early 30s.

Figure 2-2. Percentage change in school-age (5- to 14-year-old) population between 2000 and 2015, selected African countries

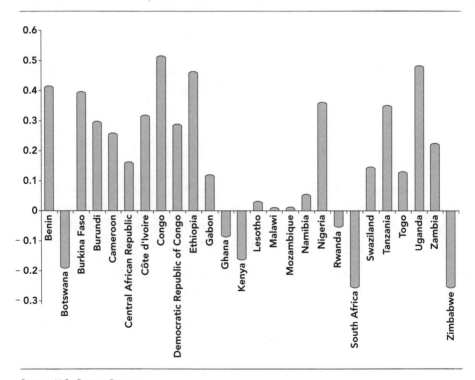

Source: U.S. Census Bureau.

HIV/AIDS may have an important impact on enrollment rates. While the evidence does not uniformly point to lower enrollment among AIDS orphans, demand does appear to be adversely affected among poorer families, particularly at the secondary and tertiary levels, and the epidemic makes many families poorer (World Bank 1999). In some countries orphans in foster homes may also be disadvantaged in access to education, as well as to health care and adequate nutrition (Deininger, Garcia, and Subbarao 2001). In some cases lower demand is also the result of children dying of AIDS because of mother-child transmission (estimated in Zimbabwe to be as high as 70 percent of all under-five child deaths). Generally, however, most children born uninfected are unlikely to become infected until they reach adolescence or become sexually active. Thus for most countries, increases in the school-age population are expected.

AIDS orphans

The increase in orphans may well represent one of the largest impacts of the AIDS epidemic (box 2-3). Estimated at 2 percent for Africa prior to the epidemic, the proportion of orphans to all children has now risen to as high as 15 to 20 percent in some African countries. Estimates indicate that 50 percent of these children were orphaned by AIDS.

The number of AIDS orphans in Asia is small relative to Africa, but is significant and growing. In 2000, maternal and double orphans in Thailand were estimated to number 222,716, with 20 percent of them the result of AIDS (Hunter and Williamson 2000), while AIDS orphans in India in 1999 numbered 557,570 (UNAIDS 2000b). Globally, since the beginning of the epidemic, more than 13 million children have lost their mother or both parents to AIDS, 10.4 million of them under 15 years old (UNAIDS 2000a). Many of the orphans who are alive today may themselves die of AIDS, but many will live—and demand urgent attention.

AIDS orphans are estimated to number 35 million by 2010. Projections for 1990–2010 for 15 African countries show uniformly significant increases resulting from parents' AIDS mortality (figure 2-3). Projections indicate that in 2010, 79 to 94 percent of orphans will be the result of AIDS mortality, compared with 61 to 84 percent in 2000.

Orphans are among society's most vulnerable children. They suffer the trauma of seeing their parents die of AIDS, often become "orphaned" several times over as new caretakers also become infected, fall victim to malnutrition and stunting, and risk becoming street children. Evidence from Africa is stark. A study in Côte d'Ivoire showed that when a family member had AIDS, family income fell by 52 to 67 percent and food consumption dropped by 41 percent, while in Zambia the epidemic contributed to a doubling of street children (to 75,000) between 1991 and 1996 (Gachuhi 1999; UNICEF and UNAIDS 1999).

Box 2-3. School-age orphans in Africa: How many?

The AIDS epidemic has clearly raised the number of orphaned children in hard-hit countries, but no current estimate of the number of school-age orphans due to AIDS or other causes is available. Estimates of orphan numbers depend on the definition of an orphan, the time frame, and other underlying assumptions. UNAIDS (2000a) estimates that 12.1 million children under 15 in Sub-Saharan Africa have lost their mother (maternal orphans) or both parents (double orphans) from AIDS since the beginning of the AIDS epidemic. This number thus includes children who have now died or are older than 15 and excludes children who have lost their father only (paternal orphans). Hunter and Williamson (2000) estimate that in 2000, in 26 African countries 30.4 million children aged 0 to 14 had lost their mother, father, or both parents from any cause (not only AIDS). Both the estimates are based on projection models that incorporate assumptions about the spread of HIV and the mortality rate and include children younger than school age.

Direct evidence from household surveys in the late 1990s reveals considerable differences in the proportions of school-age children who are maternal, paternal, or double orphans. Data on children aged 7 to 14 in 22 African countries show that the double orphan rate (from all causes) ranges from 0.5 to 2 percent in all but three countries, an additional 4 percent of children have lost their mother only, and two to three times that share have lost their father only (Ainsworth and Filmer forthcoming). These percentages include children orphaned from any cause.

Planning a response requires more precise information on the current and future numbers of orphans. However, for this information to be useful it is also essential to determine the importance of the loss of one or both parents for enrollment, completion, and learning outcomes relative to other factors, such as household income, school costs and quality, and labor market returns.

The impact of orphaning on school enrollment is unclear for the following reasons:

- Studies are inconclusive. Demographic and household survey data from 12 countries in Africa and Latin America found that participation in schooling was consistently lower for children who had lost both parents (UNAIDS 2000a). A subsequent analysis of such data from six African countries also showed that double orphans were substantially underenrolled in Burkina Faso, Côte d'Ivoire, and Kenya—but not in Tanzania, Uganda, or Zimbabwe. In Uganda orphan enrollment

Figure 2-3. AIDS orphans, maternal and double, as a percentage of all children under 15 years old, selected African countries and years

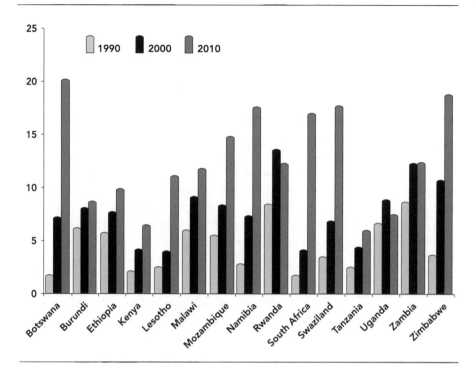

Source: Hunter and Williamson 2000.

was found to be higher than the national average. In virtually all countries orphan enrollment was strongly linked to household economic status (with the exception of Kenya, South Africa, and Uganda). In another recent analysis of 23 countries from various parts of the world, double orphanhood affected enrollment in some, but not all, countries (figure 2-4).

- Countries vary considerably in terms of overall enrollment rates, ranging from more than 90 percent to less than 30 percent. Low-enrollment countries appear to face basic educational and social constraints that prevent the enrollment of nonorphaned and orphaned children alike.

- Available evidence suggests considerable variation in the gender gap in enrollment among children with two living parents and those for whom both parents have died (figure 2-5). In most cases, the gender gap among double orphans is similar to the gender gap among children living with their parents. Important exceptions are in Cameroon, Ghana, and Kenya, where the gender gap among double orphans is larger, while in Haiti, Nigeria, and Tanzania female double orphans have higher enrollment rates than male double orphans, a reversal of the situation among nonorphans.

The message from these studies may be that the impact of orphanhood on enrollment is locally specific, and that developing an effective strategy to improve enrollment will require local understanding of the problems and a locality-specific response.

Enrollment is essential to education access, but remaining in school is equally important for learning. While little is known about the impact of orphaning on enrollment, even less is known about completion. A rare longitudinal study from Malawi found that double orphans were twice as likely to drop out of school (17.1 percent dropout rate) during the following year, compared with children with one parent dead (9.1 percent) or both parents living (9.5 percent) (Harris and Schubert 2001). In contrast, a study in northwestern Tanzania found that maternal orphans and children in households with an

Figure 2-4. Average school enrollment by orphan status, age 7 to 14 years, selected countries and years

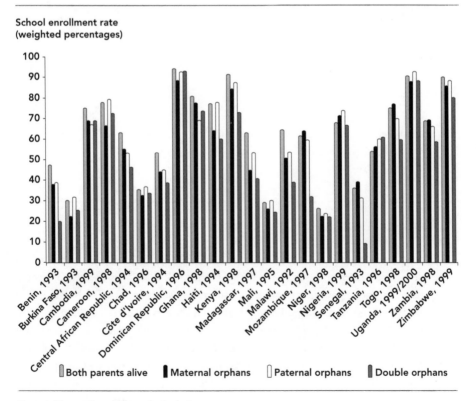

School enrollment rate (weighted percentages)

■ Both parents alive   ■ Maternal orphans   ▢ Paternal orphans   ■ Double orphans

Source: Ainsworth and Filmer, forthcoming.

Figure 2-5. School enrollment rates of male and female orphan children, age 7 to 14 years, selected countries and years

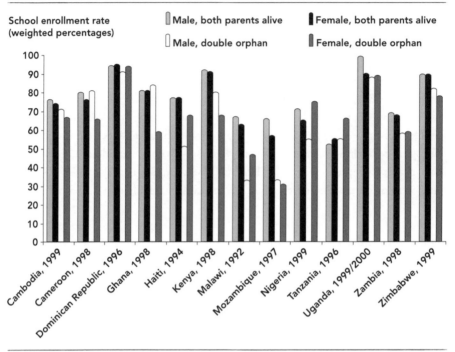

Source: Ainsworth and Filmer, forthcoming.

adult death delayed enrollment in primary school, but were not more likely to drop out of primary school once enrolled (Ainsworth, Beegle, and Koda 2001).

School-age girls

Girls and young women are highly vulnerable to HIV/AIDS (box 2-4), and a lack of education makes them more so. Girls are at greater risk than boys because of gender inequalities in status, power, and access to resources. A study in 72 capital cities (32 in Sub-Saharan Africa) showed significantly higher HIV infection rates not only for girls, but for all adults, where the gap between male and female literacy rates was larger (Over 1998). Girls are particularly vulnerable to contracting AIDS for social, cultural, economic, and even physiological reasons (figure 2-6). Greater risk arises from practices that encourage girls to accept older men as partners in preference to their peers (the "sugar daddy" syndrome); customs such as early marriage, a man's inheritance of a deceased brother's wife, some sexual practices, and abduction; child-rearing practices and initiation messages that encourage girls to be nonassertive and to accept subordinate status in relation to their husbands and other men; and social norms that inhibit girls' discussion of sexual health and accord inferior status to women. By contrast, some cultural norms can reduce girls' risk of HIV/AIDS infection, such as those of the Indian subcontinent shown to be effective in protecting girls from premarital and extramarital sex (Caldwell and others 1999).

Box 2-4. HIV/AIDS infection rates among girls and young women

In Africa
"In 11 population-based studies, the average infection rates in teenage African girls were over five times higher than those in teenage boys. Among young people in their early 20s, the rates were three times higher in women. In large measure, this enormous discrepancy is due to age-mixing between young women and older men, who have had much more sexual experience and are much more likely to be exposing the girls to HIV. It is also because girls are more easily infected during vaginal intercourse with an infected partner than are boys" (UNAIDS 2000a).

In the Caribbean
"The heterosexual epidemics of HIV infection in the Caribbean are driven by the deadly combination of early sexual activity and frequent partner exchange by young people. In Saint Vincent and the Grenadines, a quarter of men and women in a recent national survey said they had started having sex before the age of 14. A mixing of ages—which has contributed to pushing the HIV rates in young African women to such high levels—is common in this population too: while most young men had sex with women of their age or younger, over 28 percent of young girls said they had sex with older men. As a result, HIV rates are five times higher in girls than boys aged 15–19 in Trinidad and Tobago, and at one surveillance center for pregnant women in Jamaica, girls in their late teens had almost twice the prevalence rate of older women" (UNAIDS 2000a).

The epidemic also reduces girls' access to education. Girls are more likely than boys to be retained at home for domestic work when household income drops due to AIDS deaths or to care for sick relatives. Thus HIV/AIDS reduces girls' already low enrollment in secondary and tertiary education. Especially in Africa, secondary school enrollment rates, particularly for girls, are already extremely low, and the disparity between male and female enrollment in universities and colleges is also high (UNESCO 2000). With girls in secondary education more likely to contract the disease and drop out earlier than boys, the epidemic is likely worsening the gap between male and female enrollment in tertiary education.

Figure 2-6. HIV/AIDS prevalance rates for young people aged 15 to 24, by gender, selected countries, end of 1999

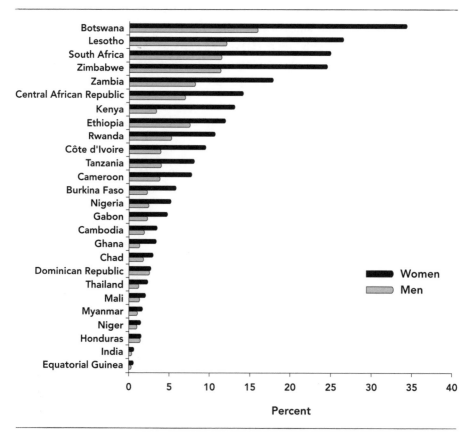

Note: Prevalance rates are given as the mid-point between the UNAIDS low and high estimates for each country.

Source: UNAIDS 2000a.

In some countries the epidemic contributes to making the education system itself a source of risk, especially for girls. While reliable data are lacking and information is largely anecdotal, abuse and harassment of school-age girls is frequently reported (box 2-5).

A recent Vatican report indicates that faith-based schools may not be an exception. An additional risk that leads parents to keep their daughters out of school relates to the harassment of girls on their way to and from school, especially where travel distances are long. Girls may also be coerced into sex in exchange for educational advancement or other favors. A study in Tanzania found that a quarter of primary school girls reported having sex with adult men, including teachers; receiving money or presents was one of the reasons for engaging in sexual activity. Twenty-two percent of primary school girls in Uganda and 50 percent in Kenya anticipate receiving gifts or money in exchange for sex (UNAIDS 2000a). Typically with older men, these sexual relations expose the girls to increased risk of HIV infection.

Box 2-5. How common is sexual abuse of children and adolescents?

- In South Africa 40–47 percent of sexual assaults are perpetrated against girls aged 15 or younger.
- In Zimbabwe 10 percent of girls, and in South Africa 30 percent, reported that their first sexual intercourse was forced.
- In rural Malawi 55 percent of adolescent girls in a survey reported being forced to have sex.
- In urban Zimbabwe half of all reported rape cases involved girls younger than 15, who were most likely to have been abused by male relatives, neighbors, or schoolteachers.
- In one Ugandan district 31 percent of schoolgirls (and 15 percent of boys) reported being sexually abused, mainly by teachers.
- In Botswana more than two-fifths of all rape cases involve girls under 16.
- In Nairobi, Kenya, one-fifth of teenage girls reported being sexually abused.
- A clinic in Harare, Zimbabwe for sexually abused children receives more than 90 children a month, half of them younger than 12.

Sources: Gachuhi 1999; UNAIDS 2000a.

This is not to imply that girls should be the target of intervention programs, but rather that interventions need to be segmented not only by age, but also by gender. Boys' behaviors expose them to specific and different risks of contracting HIV. In some countries in Asia and Africa, for example, boys typically have their first sexual intercourse with commercial sex workers, thereby increasing their risks of HIV infection. Interventions that promote male responsibility and address other risky male behavior are an essential part of the overall response to the epidemic.

Impact of HIV/AIDS on education sector costs

The specific costs of HIV/AIDS to the education sector, now beginning to be estimated, are large. With many countries providing extensive sick leave benefits to teachers, long-term absenteeism can impose a serious burden on education budgets while constraining funds for replacement teachers. In Swaziland, for example, the theoretical cost of hiring and training teachers to replace those lost to AIDS is estimated to reach US$233 million by 2016—an unsupportable cost that exceeds the total 1998-99 government budget for all goods and services (Kelly 2000a; UNAIDS 2000b). Opportunity costs should also be considered in terms of the loss of experienced teachers and education sector personnel, as well as the macroeconomic consequences of an increasing proportion of children with reduced or no access to education.

Budgets are having to accommodate higher teacher hiring and training costs (to replace the growing numbers of teachers who have died) as well as the payment of full salaries to absent—and nonperforming—teachers, with additional training and salary costs for substitute teachers where absences are official. Zambia has estimated that the epidemic's financial burden on its education sector will amount to some US$25 million between 2000 and 2010, largely reflecting the costs of increasing the supply of teachers as well as teacher absenteeism. Mozambique's estimate is about twice as much. In both cases the cost of salaries for absent teachers was some three times the cost of training to replace teachers who had died. This implies that the cost of providing substitute teachers for those who are absent is likely to be a much greater drain on budgets than the cost of training.

Distance education may be one innovative way to help contain costs. The per student cost of distance education amounts to 33 to 66 percent of that for conventional programs for teacher training, between 5 and 20 percent for some secondary education programs, and 13 to 73 percent for the tertiary level through open universities.

Current estimates of the cost of HIV/AIDS do not include demand-side costs. Efforts to ensure that orphans and other vulnerable children enroll and remain in school represent a rapidly growing new expenditure, especially in the worst-affected countries. The unit cost of supporting orphans and vulnerable children through bursaries and other incentives for fostering may be 10 times the per capita public budget for education. These costs may be borne by welfare and other systems quite separate from education, but are nevertheless likely to be important investments in ensuring that all children have access to school. There is an urgent need to assess the financial implications of the growing numbers of orphans and vulnerable children to the achievement of EFA.

The World Bank is estimating the cost of achieving EFA by 2015 in low-income countries (Mingat and Bruns 2002). As part of these analyses, a preliminary estimate has been made of the additional costs of achieving EFA that might be attributable to the impact of HIV/AIDS on education systems. This estimate is based on the following assumptions about the impact of HIV/AIDS on education supply and demand (Partnership for Child Development 2002).

The impact on education supply is assumed to be largely the cost of paying for teachers who substitute for those who are absent because of illness. This is estimated by assuming (a) that teachers are infected and affected in the same proportion as adults in general (the

HIV prevalence figures used are UNAIDS estimates between 2000 and 2015); and (b) that for an individual affected teacher the disease develops over a 10-year period on average, and during that period 260 working days (10 percent of teaching years) are lost because of absenteeism.

The impact on demand is based on the number of school-age children in the presence of HIV/AIDS and the proportion of these children who are orphans and may require additional support to attend school. The numbers of maternal and double orphans were determined for 1999 using UNAIDS estimates and projected to 2015 using a simulation model. This was done for 10 countries and then generalized to other countries in Africa by extrapolating subregional patterns for West Africa, East Africa, and southern Africa. It was assumed that the cost of supporting a maternal or double orphan to remain enrolled in school was US$50 per year (at U.S. dollar values for 2000), a cost estimate that is consistent with some recent programs in the region.

Based on these assumptions, HIV/AIDS is estimated to add between US$450 million and US$550 million per year (at U.S. dollar values for 2000, depending on other assumptions in the modeling) to the cost of achieving EFA in the 33 African countries studied. This implies that HIV/AIDS increases the total EFA financing gap for these countries by about one-third.

Apart from financial costs, major macroeconomic consequences can be expected if HIV/AIDS causes an increasing proportion of children to have reduced access or no access to education. These issues need to be fully explored for strategic and financial planning purposes.

3

Country Responses:
Promising Directions

Education ministries and their partners have had to grapple with a series of issues in the light of the diverse and egregious consequences of HIV/AIDS for the sector. Key questions in this context include the following:

- How to ensure that school-age children—often the largest uninfected group—remain uninfected as they grow up
- How to maximize prevention efforts for the highest-risk groups: girls and adolescents
- How to protect the quality and quantity of education in the face of teacher mortality and absenteeism and supply shortages, particularly in rural areas and at the postbasic level
- How to address the problem of the burgeoning numbers of orphans who could either become infected and die or who could end up out of school and on the streets
- How to find cost-effective ways of doing all of the above, given the rising costs to the sector as a result of the epidemic.

This chapter presents an overview of a range of efforts, summarized in table 3-1, that countries have been taking to address the foregoing questions. For all countries prevention is paramount. For those in or near crisis circumstances, additional efforts to bolster the supply of teachers in the short term and address the orphan situation have been essential. Some progress is being made, especially where efforts include a combination of the various approaches discussed (box 3-1).

Table 3-1. Promising approaches

Category	Target group[a]	Approach	Success factors
Efforts by all countries	• Children and youth in school, including orphans • Children and youth out of school, including orphans • Teachers and sector administrators • Parents and communities	Promotion of overall education outcomes: • Vigorous pursuit of EFA goals, including focus on girls' education • Strategic planning to estimate education system needs Prevention of HIV/AIDS among teachers and students: • School-based prevention programs • Skills-based approach ("life skills") • Focus on youth • Peer education and counseling • Multimedia campaigns • Involvement of teachers and teacher unions	• Establish high-level commitment • Catch children early, sustain efforts throughout education levels • Reform curricula to focus on behavioral change rather than mere information provision • Link school-based programs with other community-based, youth-friendly services, especially those tied to health • Heavily involve youth, communities, parents, and teachers; also recognize need for partnership with private sector, nongovernmental organizations, government
Incremental efforts by worst-affected countries		• Support for orphans and other vulnerable children • Support for out-of-school youth • Efforts to maintain supply (by increasing output from teacher training colleges, distance education)	• Adopt participatory approaches • Integrate interventions across sectors to ensure, for example, that education is provided in a clean and sanitary environment or that AIDS prevention is complemented by efforts to prevent sexually transmitted or other communicable diseases • Ensure adequate teacher training, with a focus on secondary and tertiary levels • Focus on girls • Encourage innovation, flexibility

Note: Columns are independent; no alignment across lines is intended.

a. May be further broken down, between girls and boys, and rural and urban.

Source: Authors.

Box 3-1. Progress in Zambia

The problem

Zambia is among the countries worst affected by the HIV/AIDS epidemic. In 1999 nearly 20 percent of adults 15 to 49 years old were infected. Data from recent household surveys suggest that Zambia may have some 680,000 orphans, with between 12 and 15 percent of children under 15 being one-parent or double orphans (Ainsworth and Filmer forthcoming; Hunter and Williamson 2000).

With low enrollment and high dropout rates, most children 14 years old or older are not in school (Siamwiza 1998); this is especially true of orphans. In 1999 the country was facing declines in the number of trained teachers and education officers, increased teacher absenteeism, reduced public finance for schools, more orphans with less access to education, and fewer children able to attend or complete school (Malambo 2000). HIV prevalence among primary school teachers (1996–97) is estimated at about 20 percent, and teacher death rates are about 70 percent higher than for the general population of adults (1998). The majority of trained teachers is now concentrated in urban areas, and teacher posting has been difficult. Prolonged illness and erratic attendance have caused losses in teaching time (Kelly 1999).

The response

The multisectoral National AIDS Control Program has been in place since 1992. HIV/AIDS prevention programs have been introduced throughout the education system for teacher trainees, teachers, and schoolchildren, including anti-AIDS clubs and peer-led education approaches. Efforts have also sought to reach children outside the formal education sector through more than 200 community schools. More than 80 government and nongovernment programs are targeting youth on HIV and other reproductive health matters. HIV/AIDS counseling for teachers and other educational personnel is envisaged, along with the integration of HIV/AIDS awareness into in-service training programs.

Some results

Increased awareness of HIV/AIDS in Zambia appears to have helped change behavior in some groups. A comparison of sexual behavior in 15- to 19-year-olds in 1992 and 1998 suggests a decrease in the number of sexual partners and in the proportion of young, unmarried women who were sexually active (from 52 to 35 percent). UNAIDS sentinel surveillance data from Lusaka also shows that the percentage of HIV-positive pregnant girls aged 15 to 19 has dropped by almost 50 percent in the last six years (UNAIDS 2000a).

Many challenges remain, however, including the need to equip teachers to teach HIV/AIDS prevention, the absence of links to supportive services such as youth-friendly clinics, and the lack of suitable teaching materials.

Source: Hunter and Williamson 2000; Kelly 1999; UNAIDS 2000i.

School-based prevention programs

Schools are the primary institutions able to reach the great majority of children and young people, while also having an impact at the community level. With the growing recognition that attitudes and beliefs are formed early in life, more reproductive health programs are being implemented in primary schools with the aim of reaching students before they become sexually active and, in many cases, drop out of school (because of becoming pregnant, contracting an infection, caring for a sick relative, or being orphaned). Schools also have the benefit of staff equipped with the tools of teaching and learning, and in many developing countries teachers assume an important role in the community, while also serving as role models to many adolescents. In addition, schools may often be the only place where adolescents can obtain accurate information on reproductive health. A study in Vietnam, for example, found teenagers complaining that discussions with adults about HIV/AIDS often focused on morality rather than on the practicalities of prevention.

School-based reproductive health programs vary greatly between and within countries. Programs could include one or more of these elements: family life or life skills education, sex education, HIV/AIDS education, and school-based health services. With the spread of AIDS long-standing taboos on sex education are beginning to be relaxed. According to some researchers, most countries are seeking to develop school-based AIDS education as part of their wider public education strategies. In Zimbabwe subjects once avoided are now discussed frankly in the context of HIV/AIDS prevention. In Trinidad and Tobago a survey of youths showing gross misinformation about AIDS prevention led to the recommendation to add a comprehensive HIV/AIDS education program to secondary school curricula.

Knowledge about how HIV/AIDS is transmitted can be embedded in the science curriculum. In countries where the curriculum is already overloaded, integrating new themes into existing subjects may be more effective than adding new ones. The issues surrounding HIV/AIDS can also be addressed in civics, social studies, and "moral education" curricula. Recognizing and respecting diversity, and respecting and valuing all people as full individuals, can be powerful antidotes to the stigmatization of people affected and infected by HIV/AIDS.

Skills-based health education

School-based approaches—presented throughout the remainder of this paper—often incorporate a skills-based approach to health education. Such education seeks to go beyond the provision of information about issues such as sex, sexually transmitted diseases (STDs), and HIV (transmission, risk factors, how to avoid infection), which by itself is insufficient to bring about behavioral change (Hubley 2000). Skills-based health education aims to help children develop the knowledge, attitudes, values, and skills— including interpersonal skills, critical and creative thinking, decisionmaking, and self-awareness—needed to make sound health-related decisions.

According to major reviews covering 23 studies in the United States (Kirby and others 1994); 53 studies in Europe, the United States, and elsewhere (UNAIDS 1997a); and 37 studies in other countries, including in Asia and Latin America (UNAIDS 1999b):

- School-based HIV/AIDS prevention adopting a life skills approach to health education is effective.
- Behavior change is possible if programs focus on specific behavioral goals, provide sufficient training and support for teachers, and use an age-appropriate and gender-sensitive design.
- Program impact occurs slowly and is significant, but not large. For example, AIDS prevention campaigns in Switzerland helped reduce the share of sexually active 17-year-old boys from 65 percent in 1985 to 54 percent in 1997, while the share of sexually active 15-year-old boys in the United States fell from 33 percent in 1988 to 25 percent in 1995 (UNAIDS 2000a). Note, however, that for the worst-affected countries and those with large populations, relatively small and slow changes in behavior could save the lives of millions of children.

These studies are encouraging. In addition, a recent evaluation of an intensive, two-year, school-based health education program in Uganda—among the worst-affected countries— found that the share of students in their last year of primary school who reported being sexually active dropped from 42.9 percent in 1996 to 11.1 percent two years later. A control group exposed only to the national health education curriculum showed no significant decline during the same period (Shuey and others 1999). Also heartening, extensive data now confirm that effective life skills programs promote abstinence and help children and adolescents to delay first sex (Fawole and others 1999; Gachuhi 1999; Hubley 2000; UNAIDS 1997b), thereby providing a definitive response to those who argue that reproductive health programs for children may encourage promiscuity. One point worth noting is the lack of broad evidence on the success of the skills-based approach in Africa, under-scoring the need for greater monitoring and evaluation of the impact of interventions in the continent most gravely affected by the epidemic.

Some examples of skills-based education programs from around the world follow.

Caribbean

The Health and Family Life Education program seeks to empower students to promote behavioral change. A proactive approach, it includes providing information on such topics as HIV/AIDS, sexual health, substance abuse, environmental health, safety, and nutrition. Students are empowered with skills, values, attitudes, and knowledge, and enact real-life situations in class. Sponsoring partners—Caribbean Economic Community (CARICOM) ministers of education and health, the University of the West Indies, the Pan American Health Organization/World Health Organization (WHO), and several United Nations (U.N.) agencies—plan to implement a strategy to strengthen the program in CARICOM states.

India

The pioneering Better Life Options Program in India, implemented by the Centre for Development and Population Activities, uses an empowerment model that offers adolescent girls a combination of life skills, including literacy and vocational training, support for entering and staying in formal school, family life education, and leadership training. A holistic approach integrates education, livelihoods, and reproductive health. A cross-sectional study covering peri-urban Delhi, rural Madhya Pradesh, and rural Gujarat showed that the Better Life Options Program has a significant impact on participants' economic empowerment (literacy, completion of secondary education, employment, and vocational skills), autonomous decisionmaking (when to marry, how to spend money), reproductive health (visits to health centers alone, knowledge of HIV/AIDS), self-esteem and confidence, and child survival practices.

Peru

A skills-based education program on sexuality and HIV/AIDS prevention in secondary school was found to have a significant effect on knowledge about sexuality and AIDS, sexuality, acceptance of contraception, tolerance of people with AIDS, and prevention-oriented behaviors. The program was facilitated by trained teachers and implemented over seven weekly two-hour sessions, with homework promoting interaction with family, friends, and local health institutions (Caceres and others 1994).

Uganda

Uganda's experience with a skills-based approach offers some important lessons. After a school health education program yielded little progress in attitudes and behavioral change, a life skills program for primary and secondary schools was piloted in 1994. A year later no improvement had been realized, because teachers lacked confidence in using new participatory teaching methods, were uneasy and afraid (for social, religious, or work reasons) to cover topics of sexuality and condom use, and perceived this subject to be relatively unimportant (given the absence of examinations). Recognizing the need for greater commitment and cooperation, the ministry of education has responded with a new curriculum and improved teacher training approaches (Gachuhi 1999), and Uganda's AIDS Commission reports a fall in the rate of new infections of almost 50 percent among 15- to 19-year-olds.

Vietnam

According to evaluations, a skills-based HIV/AIDS prevention program launched in 1997 has increased schoolchildren's knowledge of HIV/AIDS and how to avoid contracting it, and also improved their tolerance and decisionmaking skills. Teachers' knowledge also improved, while a UNAIDS evaluation found that the program was effective in building students' and teachers' confidence. The pilot life skills approach was implemented in schools, with teacher training and a focus on student knowledge, attitudes, values, and behaviors (UNAIDS 2000d).

Zimbabwe

The AIDS Action Program for Schools initiated by the ministry of education and culture in 1992 in collaboration with the United Nations Children's Fund (UNICEF) has also not yielded impressive results. The program targets students and teachers in all primary (grades 1 to 6) and secondary (grades 4 to 7) schools in an attempt to develop their problem solving, decisionmaking, and risk averting skills. More than 2,000 teachers from over 6,000 schools have been trained; the program possesses textbooks and learning materials; and has the full support of the government, churches, and other influential groups (Gachuhi 1999; Gatawa 1995). A 1995 review found that only a third of teachers had received in-service training, that teachers were unfamiliar with the new participatory techniques, and that they found topics of sex and HIV embarrassing and difficult to teach.

In the 1990s Zimbabwe developed the Auntie Stella health education pack for secondary school students. Auntie Stella is a classroom-based pack of question and answer cards that address students' concerns or gaps in knowledge (identified through up-front participatory research) on reproductive health, including rape, sexual harassment, STDs, AIDS, unwanted pregnancy, and lack of money leading to commercial sex. Students analyze behaviors and participate in exercises to devise action plans for behavioral change and risk reduction. Following field testing in eight pilot schools, Auntie Stella will be expanded to the national level (Ndlovu and Kaim 1999).

A recent multisectoral, multipartner school initiative merits special attention. Known as Focusing Resources on Effective School Health (FRESH), it uses the skills-based approach to HIV/AIDS prevention (box 3-2). FRESH is a partnership of WHO, UNICEF, United Nations Educational, Scientific, and Cultural Organization (UNESCO), Education International, the World Food Program, the World Bank, and others launched at the Education for All (EFA) Forum in Dakar, Senegal, in April 2000. It seeks to improve learning and educational outcomes by enhancing the health of schoolchildren and provides a useful planning framework to help countries develop health components within their national education programs. The framework includes health-related school policies, provision of safe water and adequate sanitation in schools, skills-based health education, and school-based health and nutrition services. The aim is to implement all these components together in every school so that they create an environment that promotes learning and attendance. Skills-based education aims to delay first sex, encourage abstinence, and promote condom use. Students acquire skills needed for positive behavioral change, including interpersonal communication, value clarification, decisionmaking, negotiation, goal setting, self-assertion, and stress management. Core activities, which involve communities, teachers, health workers, and students, focus on four priorities: skills-based education for HIV/AIDS prevention, school health policies on HIV/AIDS discrimination, a healthy school environment, and school-based counseling and health clubs for HIV/AIDS.

Box 3-2. Why FRESH?

- FRESH ensures better educational outcomes. Ensuring good health while children are of school age can boost enrollment and attendance, reduce the need for repetition, and increase educational attainment.
- FRESH improves social equity. Strategies for universal basic education give the most disadvantaged children—girls, poor rural children, children with disabilities—access to school for the first time. These are the children who will benefit the most from health interventions.
- FRESH is a highly cost-effective strategy. School health programs help link resources for health, education, nutrition, and sanitation to an infrastructure (the school) that is already in place; the school system has an extensive, skilled work force that already works closely with the community.

Using peer educators and counselors

Peer education has been a component of HIV/AIDS prevention efforts for the last decade. Young people are often more comfortable discussing such matters as HIV/AIDS and sex with peer educators and counselors (for example, respected students, colleagues, or neighbors) than "outsiders" or authority figures. Peer groups often begin to take on more importance during adolescence, and identification with peer educators enables individuals to discuss sexual issues with less embarrassment. As a Jamaican student put it: "Our thoughts are basically the same and I feel much better discussing the subject of sex with my peers" (Family Health International 1996). Peer education, which increasingly has the objective of behavioral change rather than mere information exchange, can include group or individual informal discussions, video and drama presentations, and recreational activities that extend beyond the classroom.

Qualitative information indicates that peer education and counseling are helping school health programs in many countries. In Kenya, such a program in nine institutions of higher education has reached 19,000 students and substantially increased their access to sexual and reproductive health services and information (UNAIDS 2000d). The program supported the creation of AIDS awareness clubs whose activities include condom distribution and newsletters. In Asia, the Asian Red Cross/Red Crescent initiated the Youth Peer Education Program on reproductive health, STDs, and HIV/AIDS in 1994. Taken up by 12 participating countries (Cambodia, China, India, Indonesia, the Republic of Korea, the Lao People's Democratic Republic, Malaysia, Myanmar, Nepal, the Philippines, Thailand, and Vietnam), the program has delivered education about reproductive health, STDs, and HIV/AIDS to more than 42,000 youth. A recent survey of HIV/AIDS peer education programs underscores the need to integrate them with other interventions—such as condom distribution, medical care, voluntary counseling, and HIV testing—and to ensure peer educator training in participatory techniques aimed at problem solving and behavioral change.

Planning for the supply of teachers

Projecting the future needs of the education sector is an essential component of education planning, whether or not a country is in the grip of the epidemic. Specific planning tools are helping countries estimate the impact of HIV/AIDS on the supply of teachers. Four countries in Africa, for example, have used World Bank–furnished models to project the disease's impact on education supply and demand. In Zambia, projections to 2010 have been made for teacher availability and the number of children requiring education: assuming a primary student-to-teacher ratio of 46:1, a deficit of approximately 3,900 teachers is expected. These conclusions assume current low enrollment rates and high dropout rates, especially for orphans and girls. If a higher share of children were to attend school, reflecting EFA objectives, the teacher-student gap would be even larger, and greater efforts would be required to enhance supply. Box 3-3 offers another example of strategic planning to mitigate the impact of HIV/AIDS on education systems.

Box 3-3. Strategic planning for education in southern Africa

The primary goal of the Southern African Mobile Task Team on HIV/AIDS in Education (MTT), established in 2000 in the University of Natal, South Africa, is to help education ministries develop strategic plans to mitigate the impact of HIV/AIDS on education systems. Using a systematic approach to management, MTT approaches HIV/AIDS as a strategic development issue for African education. It is funded by the U.S. Agency for International Development, which also helped create and develop the concept.

MTT has worked in Malawi, Namibia, and Zambia, and is initiating activity in Ethiopia and South Africa. It has also opened a dialogue with the 16 countries of the West Africa Economic Community.

MTT helps countries produce detailed reports of the current impact of HIV/AIDS on education and the government's response to date, using its own tools, techniques, templates, and models (rapid appraisal frameworks, objective and vision-setting techniques, prioritization planning, teacher demand and supply modeling, district-level data collection systems, partnership database development, and analysis of technical assistance requirements). The process aims at a shared vision for the future; consensus on prioritized goals to achieve this vision; and a detailed, achievable action plan with dates and allocation of responsibilities. These elements provide the basis for reporting to the public and for future planning.

Since November 2000, the Education and HIV/AIDS (Ed-SIDA/AIDS) initiative has been helping governments project and respond to the impact of HIV/AIDS on their efforts to achieve EFA. Jointly developed by the World Bank, the United Kingdom's Department for International Development (DfID), the International Institute for Educational Planning, and the Partnership for Child Development, the initiative trains education planners in developing and using country-specific models that provide quantitative input into the planning process by projecting the impact of HIV/AIDS on education supply and demand. Each model tracks the number of teachers by age, sex, and HIV status; annual recruitment and retirement rates; and number of teachers leaving the profession (box 3-4). Demand projections for education rely on trends in female AIDS mortality rates, age-specific female fertility rates, and survival estimates for HIV-negative and HIV-positive children. The share of school-age children who have lost their mother or both parents to AIDS is projected to rise in all countries analyzed. The supply and demand relationship is then used to estimate the number of teachers needed to meet EFA targets.

Box 3-4. The Ed-SIDA/AIDS model: An example

The incidence of HIV among teachers by age and sex is defined by a model that takes as input country-specific estimates of adult HIV prevalence, which are assumed to be the same as for teachers. The prevalence of HIV among new teachers can be obtained from these prevalence estimates, accounting for the age distribution of new teachers. Putting these processes together, HIV/AIDS may be seen to act on teacher supply at two levels, directly through AIDS mortality of teachers, and indirectly through the attrition of skilled workers in the general population and the subsequent attraction of teachers to these newly vacated posts. The first figure provides an example of the projected numbers of teachers in with and without HIV/AIDS epidemic scenarios for a West African country. The projection clearly shows a significant difference between the projected numbers of teachers in the presence and in the absence of HIV/AIDS: in the presence of HIV/AIDS there is a consistent and growing decline in teacher numbers.

Projected number of teachers in "with" and "without" HIV/AIDS scenarios for a West African country

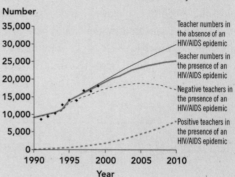

Projected numbers of school-age (age 6 to 14) maternal AIDS orphans in 2010 and comparisons with 2000 estimates of all orphans, selected African countries

Country	Number of school-age maternal AIDS orphans, 2010		Ratio of projected numbers of maternal AIDS orphans in 2010 to estimates of all orphans in 2000	
	High	Low	High	Low
Benin	80,000	53,000	5.0	3.3
Burkina Faso	391,000	156,000	4.1	1.6
Gambia, The	10,000	7,000	4.8	3.3
Ghana	228,000	96,000	3.4	1.4
Guinea	69,000	28,000	3.6	1.5
Niger	114,000	51,000	4.7	3.9
Nigeria	2,436,000	835,000	6.3	2.2
Senegal	128,000	16,000	16.0	2.0
Togo	136,000	69,000	6.9	2.0

The impact of HIV/AIDS on orphan numbers

The table shows the estimated numbers of school-age children in 2010 who will have lost their mother or both parents to AIDS. The countries produced these figures using HIV prevalence data from UNAIDS, demographic data from the UN Population Division, and fertility data from the Demographic and Health Surveys of Macro International. Numbers are projected assuming a high or low incidence of HIV.

Additional recruitment needed each year to reach 2010 targets, high and low prevalence scenarios, selected African countries

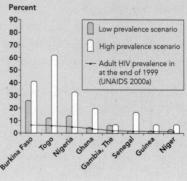

The Ed-SIDA/AIDS initiative: The impact of HIV/AIDS on efforts to achieve universal basic education

The second figure shows the projected percentage of additional recruitment necessary each year because of the impact of HIV/AIDS if country-specific targets for the number of primary-level teachers in 2010 are to be reached. These projections were made by the education planners in each of the countries listed.

Source: Partnership for Child Development 2002.

Education planners in some of the most seriously affected countries, such as Zambia, are beginning to use the Ed-SIDA/AIDS approach. However, other countries in Africa, particularly in West Africa—which has so far escaped the worst of the epidemic—and countries in other parts of the world also face the imminent prospect of an HIV/AIDS epidemic. Proactive planning and action that relies on a country-specific, HIV demographic projection model, could help reverse a potentially worsening scenario. To date, nine countries in West Africa (Benin, Burkina Faso, The Gambia, Ghana, Guinea, Niger, Nigeria, Senegal, and Togo) and Zambia are partners in the Ed-SIDA/AIDS initiative, but no country outside Africa is participating.

Maintaining the supply of teachers

The worst-affected countries have an immediate need to replace teachers, while all countries have a longer-term need to ensure the stability and quality of the supply of teachers. The most basic need is to equip teachers with the knowledge and skills to help themselves avoid HIV infection, combined with strengthening links with health services to ensure that teachers receive appropriate care and support. Fundamentally, the issue of maintaining supply is no different from the normal need for schools to provide emergency coverage for absent teachers. What is different is that the demand for coverage exceeds the available supply of qualified substitutes.

To increase supply in the short term some countries are rehiring retired teachers, combining classes, and shortening teaching time. A few education systems are even turning to pupils for some forms of peer education. In Botswana, for example, 12 percent of teachers are temporary and untrained, reflecting efforts to keep schools open, albeit with clear implications for deteriorating quality. Teacher absenteeism is a particular problem in secondary schools, given the need for specialized subject matter teaching. Some countries, including Botswana and Malawi, are considering changing teacher training curricula for secondary school teachers to cover a wider range of subjects.

The following longer-term options for ensuring teacher supply are not specific to HIV/AIDS, but include approaches that should already be in place to achieve EFA targets. What is different is that countries already stretched to achieve these goals will require an even greater effort to counter the impact of HIV/AIDS.

First, some countries are focusing efforts on increasing the output from teacher training colleges to maintain supply. Guinea, for example, still striving to achieve universal coverage, has reduced the length of the training syllabus and achieved a more than 10-fold increase in output from training colleges. Zambia has almost doubled the training output by modifying the teacher development course so that the second year of training is spent in schools rather than in colleges. These efforts could help ensure the quantity of supply, but risk compromising educational quality. By contrast, South Africa and some other countries are closing colleges because they appear to have met their immediate needs for teachers.

Second, countries are increasingly turning to distance education to increase the supply of teachers. Distance education programs are now used worldwide for teacher development and have proven effective in countries as diverse as India and Jamaica. The World Bank's "Distance Education Strategy Paper for Africa" (World Bank 2001d) notes growing efforts to improve pre-service and in-service teacher development programs. Accounting for more than half the distance education courses offered in Africa, teacher training has been found to be both economically and educationally effective (Perraton 1997). In a few cases countries are also using distance education to extend access to primary education, for instance, the interactive radio instruction model has achieved national coverage in AIDS-affected Lesotho and South Africa. At the secondary level, distance education is widely available, with some programs more than 20 years old, while almost all countries—including most in Africa—have at least one distance education program at the tertiary level.

Third, some countries have been recruiting foreign personnel to supplement local teachers. In Botswana, for example, 6 percent of all teachers are foreign contract teachers, most of them from neighboring countries, especially Zambia. This movement reflects differential financial rewards across countries and, with the growing need to retain teachers, may imply a need to supply incentives for teachers to remain in their home countries. The future supply of teachers from other traditional sources, for example, India, is likely to be increasingly compromised by HIV/AIDS.

Adopting multimedia approaches

Soul City is a dynamic and innovative South African health project that uses a multimedia approach to fight HIV/AIDS, with proven results (from independent evaluations) in advancing knowledge about AIDS and changing attitudes and social norms toward safer sexual behaviors. The project is funded by the South African government, corporate sponsors, the European Union, UNICEF, UNESCO, the DfID, the Japanese government, and the Radda Barren and Kagiso Trust. Soul City focuses on AIDS and youth sexuality themes presented through multiple vehicles, including a prime time television series; a daily radio drama; booklets and other materials on health, adult education, and life skills; and a publicity campaign. Mirroring Soul City is *Heart and Soul*, a Kenyan soap opera that will begin radio and television broadcasts and street theater performances in early 2002, and will cover such "edutainment" themes as promiscuity, poverty reduction, and human rights. The program is supported by 24

U.N. agencies, the British Council, the World Bank, the International Monetary Fund, and the Ford Foundation. Involvement by the private sector is also being sought to promote the program's sustainability over a three- to five-year period.

Interventions that promote male responsibility and address risky male behavior are urgently needed, but relatively few examples are available. A multimedia regional example that addresses this issue is the feature film *Yellow Card,* funded by the DfID, the Ford Foundation, the U.S. Agency for International Development, and Pathfinder International. The film addresses male responsibility, risky sexual behavior, and other life skills issues. It was filmed in Zimbabwe, and the script was written and acted by young people. It has been translated into French, Portuguese, Pidgin, Swahili, and several other African languages, and is being distributed as a video across Africa. The film is accompanied by training materials that help inform and provoke discussion among youth.

Supporting orphans and other vulnerable children

Ensuring that orphans and other vulnerable children receive an education presents one of the greatest challenges to governments, nongovernmental organizations (NGOs), donor agencies, and local communities in achieving EFA and Millennium Development Goals. An important step at the global level was the launch of the Hope for African Children Initiative in October 2001, an international effort that targets the continent's orphans. With a fundraising goal of US$100 million, and having already received a US$10 million, three-year grant from the Bill and Melinda Gates Foundation and the endorsement of UNICEF, the World Bank, and others, this initiative aims to build awareness and ensure the future of affected children by securing their access to health and education after their parents die. HIV/AIDS is one of many elements impeding these children's access to education. General efforts are of three kinds: to achieve EFA targets, to improve education access for all orphans and other vulnerable children, and to mitigate the impact of HIV/AIDS.

Efforts to achieve universal access to education are almost always based in the education sector and encompass formal, nonformal, informal, and popular education. Achieving EFA will require an intensified effort and will demand strategies that strengthen current education infrastructures, support strong community involvement, and rethink the ways in which the poorest and most disadvantaged children can be educated. HIV/AIDS is likely to affect how much, rather than what, needs to be done. Listed below are some key strategies (see World Bank 2001b for details):

■ To increase access to the formal system, Malawi and Uganda have eliminated primary school enrollment fees (for up to four children per household). Enrollment

Box 3-5. Helping out-of-school youth in the Philippines

The Philippine Out-of-School Children and Youth Development Project has realized positive results in a pilot effort to test some innovative approaches. Implemented in the late 1990s, the project made significant progress in providing learning opportunities to out-of-school children (6- to 14-years old) and youth (15- to 24-years old), or preparing 16- to 24-year-old high school dropouts for employment or self-employment, building the capacity of selected organizations to implement projects for out-of-school youth, and developing a basic life skills competency resource book–teaching guide for high school dropouts who undertake technical or "alternative" education. Highlights include the following:

- A partnership between the government, civil society, and the business sector that recognizes that no single sector commands the needed resources, expertise, community experience, and commitment, with some 200 local partners, including beneficiaries and their families, providing cash or in-kind support to 26 subprojects
- A target group of children and youth from low-income families who are basic education dropouts; are not formally employed; and have few opportunities to acquire basic education, life skills competencies, and employment
- A set of subprojects, including formal basic education (including life skills training), an alternative learning system (allowing for greater flexibility through a free, home or community-based delivery system with self-paced learning), and technical education (preparing typically postsecondary youth to become technicians or paraprofessionals, with a life skills element that instills values and builds self-image)
- The increase in hiring (as a result of the project) by the business sector of high school graduates who have successfully completed training and meet job requirements, with many high school dropouts who have completed in-center training demonstrating as much skill and responsibility as high school graduates
- The recognition of the importance of family through their inclusion in subprojects of support services for out-of-school-youth families
- The learning of key lessons, including that youth participation is crucial to success and that further efforts are needed to ensure the sustainability and scaling-up of such an approach.

rates are up, but the costs of uniforms, books, and materials remain an issue. Zambia still levies fees, but orphans are eligible for a subsidy.

■ Some countries have community schools, established by local communities—often with NGO support—to benefit the nonformal sector. Typically neither fees nor uniforms are required, local people serve as voluntary teachers, and timing of teaching can be adjusted to local needs; however, quality may suffer.

■ As noted earlier, distance learning using media such as radio is an option increasingly used for educating out-of-school children and youth. Distance education for primary school children is rare, but has been used in Africa in a mentored group setting for primary-school-age children in eight countries, reaching a national scale in three countries.

Efforts to help orphans and vulnerable children gain access to education are hindered by a lack of experience and poor understanding of the major constraints. While many programs are managed outside the education sector, the education sector has a specific role to play in identifying at-risk children; monitoring their participation in education; and providing fee waivers and other subsidies, as in Zimbabwe. A recent analysis of good practices in providing social protection for Africa's orphans and vulnerable children (Subbarao, Mattimore, and Plengemann 2001) concludes that the numbers are already so large as to threaten traditional coping mechanisms, and calls for strong public intervention, carefully chosen to address the specific risks orphans in a given country face and to strengthen (rather than supplant) existing community coping strategies. An innovative approach to addressing issues affecting out-of-school children and youth comes from the Philippines (box 3-5).

A World Bank, ACTAfrica analysis (2001) estimates the cost of scaling up HIV/AIDS prevention support for orphans throughout Sub-Saharan Africa at US$162 million to US$267 million, noting that

■ Subsidies for vulnerable children not in school offer four benefits:
  ▶ They are easy to monitor and less prone to abuse or fraud.
  ▶ They enable orphans to attend school when school fees are prohibitive.
  ▶ In the short term, orphans are better integrated socially into the local community.
  ▶ In the long term, orphans gain marketable skills and become productive members of society.

■ Subsidies for vulnerable children already in school allow foster families to save on education costs and increase their consumption of other goods and services. School subsidies have been used successfully in many countries to meet other goals, for example, increasing girls' access to education under Brazil's Bolsa Escola program, and are being evaluated in Zimbabwe's Basic Education Assistance Module.

■ School subsidies can be designed to address two concerns:

▶ To minimize stigma, assistance can be provided to foster parents not only for the orphan, but also for up to two other children, on the condition that all three attend school.

▶ To compensate for the loss of the child's labor at home, an additional food grant may be provided to poorer households identified at community meetings.

■ The sustainability of subsidies would be an issue for Sub-Saharan Africa where, especially in areas devastated by AIDS, local municipal funding of education grants and school subsidies (as in much of Latin America) would largely not be feasible.

HIV/AIDS-specific activities in support of orphans and other vulnerable children are largely intersectoral. There is a specific need to reduce the stigmatization and exclusion of children infected or affected by HIV/AIDS. The formal adoption of specific policies by the government, especially in the education sector, and the development of a national communication strategy aimed at teachers, parents, and the wider community, can help create a supportive environment. Another important intersectoral activity is to help delay the orphanhood and abandonment of children by ensuring that health services provide care and support for parents and caregivers living with HIV/AIDS.

4

Strategy for Action

A broad strategic response rooted in education—and set within a national, multisectoral context—is essential for all countries. Responses to the HIV/AIDS epidemic have too often been piecemeal, small-scale, health-focused, and weakly integrated into related efforts. Strong political commitment is key to addressing such shortcomings. Particularly in low-prevalence countries, governments need to recognize early on that complacency can be disastrous. A successful response will also require flexibility and creativity to meet the challenges of a sector in flux and constructive engagement with key stakeholders, such as communities, religious leaders, educators, and politicians, who have influence—and often conflicting points of view.

A commitment to overall education goals in the HIV/AIDS context also requires an understanding of why stand-alone, preventive education programs provide only a partial response to the problem. Important as they are, these programs face a number of challenges. Those children most in need of such education are often dropouts, and will thus not be reached. In addition, prevention messages are rendered ineffective by teachers who are uncommitted, uneasy, or poorly informed about such topics, or by students' lack of access to related health services. Perhaps most important, the setting in which prevention programs are offered is often handicapped by such problems as overcrowding, lack of safety, poor classroom facilities and teaching materials, and low teacher compensation. Emphasis on general—beyond preventive—education is also important insofar as some communities and educators fear, albeit wrongly, that preventive education leads to increased sexual activity.

Define objectives and targeted outcomes

The starting point for an effective response is the affirmation of EFA goals and the express recognition that the education sector could be fortified to become a country's strongest weapon against HIV/AIDS—or failing that, its worst victim, reversing decades of hard-won gains (table 4-1). Equally important is the need to establish key, monitorable outcomes, so that progress in universal completion of primary education and gender equity in schooling, as well as prevalence and mortality goals related to the epidemic, can be measured. Foremost among the internationally agreed-on goals at the U.N. General Assembly Session in July 2001 was a 25 percent reduction in HIV infection rates among 15- to 24-year-olds in the worst-affected countries by 2005 and globally by 2010.

Table 4-1. Key objectives and outcomes

Item	*Achieve Education for All goals*	*Use education to curb HIV/AIDS*
Key objectives	• Pursue long-term human and economic development • Empower girls and women	• Adapt curricula to bring about behavioral change (long-term) • Take advantage of education system infrastructure as a vehicle for anti-AIDS efforts (short-term)
Key outcomes	• Universal completion of primary schooling by 2015 • Elimination of gender disparities in primary and secondary schooling by 2005	• 25 percent reduction in HIV prevalence among 15- to 24-year-olds (by 2005 in worst-affected countries, by 2010 in other countries)

Source: Authors.

While a national HIV/AIDS program requires multiple components for success, it must recognize the unique links between the epidemic and the education sector. HIV/AIDS is a major obstacle to the achievement of universal basic education of good quality and equitable access to education, and can easily reverse decades of hard-won gains in the sector—as has already occurred with life expectancy and child mortality. The achievement of Education for All (EFA) and gender equity goals at the same time promises to be among the most powerful means of HIV/AIDS prevention.

However, helping children, especially girls, enroll and complete schooling beyond the primary level is also important. Secondary school education is what really makes a difference to increasing age at marriage, delaying first sexual encounters, improving negotiation for protected sex, and promoting other risk-reducing behaviors. Ensuring girls' access to secondary school is also key to better employment opportunities for women, and often an opportunity to break the cycle of poverty and reduce the risk of exposure to HIV.

Expand knowledge base for interventions

Once countries have identified key objectives and outcomes, a second step within a systematic approach could be to identify where action is most urgently needed and to what extent ongoing approaches are realizing success. To that end, a country may

- Identify at-risk groups, such as orphan girls and adolescents, as well as other stake-holders, to strengthen program implementation or mobilize resources.
- Estimate the impact of HIV/AIDS on prospects for achieving EFA targets using such planning tools as the Education and HIV/AIDS (Ed-SIDA/AIDS) model. For the worst-affected countries this step is crucial for developing an emergency response, managing resources, and planning for the future, and for other countries it permits risk management and data-driven planning and decisionmaking.
- Take stock of ongoing anti-AIDS efforts within the country with a view to replicating successes and avoiding pitfalls based on lessons learned.
- Conduct operational research and impact evaluation.

Identify actions needed

Based on the crucial and unique role that education can play, this paper urges countries to

- Pursue EFA goals vigorously, including efforts to improve the quality of education, strengthen public and private institutions, and address delivery issues.
- Integrate anti-AIDS efforts into broader education efforts using promising approaches found to work within the country, and inspired by cross-country experience (see chapter 3).
- Ensure the provision of support for orphans and other vulnerable children.
- Prioritize girls' education at all levels. Girls have a higher incidence of infection than

boys, and the differential benefits accruing to educated girls have been clearly demonstrated.

■ Address the epidemic's immediate effects on the education sector in the worst-affected countries, including actions to ensure an adequate supply and quality of teachers.

For worst-affected countries, an immediate need is to implement mitigating activities to sustain the education system. Existing efforts to achieve EFA will need to be intensified, and their scope broadened. Supply-side efforts will likely call for increasing the output of teacher training colleges; rethinking plans to close colleges; and enhancing the use of distance education methods for teacher training and for education in general, particularly at the secondary and tertiary levels. Sectoral responses to address demand-side issues could include efforts to increase access to education (community schools, distance learning, abolition of fees); ensure that orphans and other vulnerable children have access to schools or to education outside schools; and undertake specific HIV/AIDS-targeted responses, for example, improving access to health services for parents and caregivers and ensuring that those infected and affected by HIV/AIDS are not excluded from education by stigmatization and prejudice.

Countries will need to ensure adequate coverage for all at-risk target groups. For example, while authorities are much more likely to establish programs for in-school children than those out of school, such interventions could well be too small in scale to make a dent in a huge national problem. In addition, where large numbers of children are out of school, education ministries would need to collaborate with other actors to explore the best options for reaching these children. Where public opinion or religious leaders frown on prevention efforts that are known to be effective (sex education and condom distribution), actors will need to be flexible, sensitive, creative, and persistent to find sustainable solutions. Where risk-avoiding behavior is inculcated into women, a corresponding effort is needed—via the community—to ensure a similar behavior change among men. At the same time, boys' education will need to promote responsible behavior on their part, along with a thorough awareness of the physical and social consequences of their actions. Another crucial issue relates to cost-effectiveness: policymakers will need to identify and adopt those approaches that have the greatest impact per unit of outlay.

For all countries the need for school-based prevention programs is paramount, with an emphasis on curriculum reform to achieve behavioral change and on expanded coverage to reach all children and youth. These programs can learn from the experience of governments and of the United Nations Population Fund, United Nations Children's Fund (UNICEF), and other organizations involved in family life education. Prevention is most effective when combined with broader health promotion efforts, and in the worst-affected countries when closely aligned with peer and other counseling services. Among the most cost-effective targets for prevention programs are youth in secondary and tertiary institutions, as they are both particularly vulnerable and particularly valuable in terms of their future contributions to society. A special focus on teacher training and development and on curricula will be crucial in equipping teachers and education administrators with the knowledge, attitudes, values, and skills needed to protect themselves and their families from HIV/AIDS. Education sectors will also need to ensure that policies and actions that support HIV/AIDS-affected teachers and administrators are in place.

While it is crucial for each country to identify the approaches that are working within its own borders, and while few evaluation-based lessons learned are available yet, some broad observations are possible based on the experience of school-based HIV/AIDS prevention strategies to date, namely:

- Skills-based health education can promote behavioral change, particularly if presented within a broadly based approach to school health and skills for life, such as Focusing Resources on Effective School Health (FRESH).
- School-based programs are likely to be more effective if linked to other youth-friendly services (including health care) in the community.
- Efforts to develop healthy behaviors should start early and be sustained throughout all levels of education.
- Parent-teacher interaction is important, as is the role of community in promoting positive cultural norms and traditional practices while addressing those that are harmful.
- Peer-based approaches offer an important alternative or supplement to student-teacher relationships.
- Secondary and tertiary levels—especially trainee teachers—merit particular attention because of the value and vulnerability of these age groups.
- Distance education approaches may be particularly relevant to the in-service training of teachers in preventive approaches.

Box 4-1 describes a program that captures many of these elements and could be a good practice model for reaching youth, but has yet to be implemented nationally. Table 4-2 takes a broader approach, identifying what education ministries could do differently in pursuit of their education goals to factor in the epidemic's impact.

Box 4-1. A youth-to-youth school health program for HIV/AIDS-affected countries in Sub-Saharan Africa

In four of Africa's worst-affected countries—South Africa, Tanzania, Uganda, and Zimbabwe—youth-driven school health programs are being delivered by trained volunteers just a few years older than the students. A creation of Students Partnership Worldwide working with education ministries, the programs are affirmative (they do not focus on ill-health) and help youth celebrate good health; uncontroversial, high profile, and supported by national figures; highly participatory, involving stakeholders ranging from government to schoolchildren; locally and community owned; holistic, and integrated with health services outside schools; built around a core component focused on addressing threats to young people's health; and clearly targeted, with measurable outcomes.

Key features of the youth-to-youth model are

- A focus on secondary schools to reach children just prior to and during adolescence, and on rural schools, where most of Africa's children are educated and that are less likely than urban schools to have access to health information and services
- A critical role for young people—including out-of-school youth—as educators and volunteers, based on a recognition of
  - ▶ Peer influence as the single most powerful determinant of early sexual behavior
  - ▶ Young people's openness to change, creative energy, ability to influence and serve as role models for younger age groups on sensitive issues, and eagerness to gain experience
  - ▶ Availability, in that often unemployed, young adults represent an untapped, plentiful, and dynamic resource and have proven to be excellent workers in the context of adolescent reproductive health
- Use of trained volunteers, not only to provide basic health education, but also to extend the extracurricular life of the school and involve the local community through sports or cultural activities that raise awareness of fundamental issues and provide a group, or community, focal point
- Integration of life skills into health promotion work in primary and secondary schools to develop self-awareness; resistance to peer pressure; and negotiation, critical thinking, and decisionmaking skills
- Inclusion of youth-friendly services, involving a close collaboration between schools and local health services, particularly in the worst-affected countries,

continued on next page

Box 4-1 continued

to ensure that highly vulnerable children have access to basic health services and the knowledge and confidence to make use of them

■ A recognition that programs' long-term sustainability depends on community ownership, cross-sectoral support (at the national policy and district operational levels), and private sector backing to spread the cost of national implementation.

Find public or private donor resources for financing these actions

In an environment of multiple demands on scarce donor resources, countries will be called upon not only to demonstrate a need for resources, but also to show that they are using them effectively. The accumulation of evidence that development outlays in the country, particularly in the education sector, do produce results will become important. Development effectiveness, in turn, will require a strong commitment by the leadership toward the broad objectives, ideally with the appointment of national champions; "ownership" on the part of those implementing the interventions; and strong collaboration and cross-sectoral partnerships among the various stakeholders, including parents, teachers, and students; and public, private, and nongovernmental partners. All these elements will be necessary to ensure that efforts are sustainable. Note that a strong focus on monitoring and evaluation will reap crucial rewards, both in identifying successes that may be replicated and in offering lessons emerging from negative experience. A well run education sector producing visible results will also be the best way to compete for tight national budgetary resources.

Address complex outstanding issues

In a crisis environment, complex issues are often put aside in favor of problems whose solutions appear more within reach. While this is natural, and to some extent appropriate, it is important for national authorities to work toward developing strategies to address the following issues:

■ *Orphans and other vulnerable children and youth.* A key challenge for the education sector is to reach children who are not in school, and therefore fall outside the education system infrastructure. For these children efforts to provide HIV-

Table 4-2. Factoring in AIDS: What education ministries could do differently

Item	Action
Policy	• Argue the case for education as an urgent national priority and as a "high return on investment" sector that should be adequately funded, highlighting its crucial role in HIV/AIDS prevention and the grave dangers of inaction (including setbacks on EFA). • Ensure—and enforce—policies that make schools safe havens for children, including zero tolerance of sexual harassment and other inappropriate or criminal behavior particularly on the part of teachers and school officials. • Ensure close collaboration with other sectors (especially health, communications, and ministries dealing with youth affairs), recognizing that the fight against HIV/AIDS can only be won with multisectoral efforts. • Engage in systematic planning, developing the needed skills and methods (such as the Ed-SIDA/AIDS model) and identifying key constraints to realize objectives as well as cost-effective ways to overcome the constraints. • Ensure adequate arrangements for monitoring and evaluation, to measure not only progress in education outcomes but also the impact and spread of HIV/AIDS as well as the impact of preventive measures.
Supply and quality	• Ensure adequate supply of teachers, compensating for higher teacher mortality and absenteeism by increasing teacher training rates including through greater reliance on distance education; reducing length of training courses and lowering qualification requirements while expanding in-service training to maintain quality; and recruiting teachers from nontraditional sources. • Strengthen delivery of prevention education, by expanding in-service training in this area, emphasizing participatory and other innovative teaching methods that promote teaching of life skills aimed at behavioral change, training youth (including those out of school) to be peer educators and counselors, and linking programs with health services. • Adapt curriculum and learning materials, introducing health education messages early on and sustaining them throughout the education system, and focusing health education on life skills approaches that emphasize behavioral change and which are grade- and age-specific (using the FRESH framework, for example). • Ensure adequate supply of classrooms, identifying innovative scheduling alternatives where constrained resources limit new construction (a majority of countries will continue to face increases in the number of school-age children).
Demand and access	• Redouble efforts to ensure access to and completion of girls' schooling, with attention to water and sanitation needs and particular emphasis on orphans and other vulnerable children, through bursaries and other established approaches. • Expand reliance on innovative approaches to reach out-of-school children, exploring distance education as well as community schools and other nonformal alternatives to provide education to rural or other inaccessible areas, for counteracting the flight of teachers to urban areas (partly to avail themselves of better health facilities).

Source: Authors.

prevention education will need to take place in shelters, clinics, workplaces, and on the street, that is, wherever young people congregate.

- *Cultural or religious barriers to such matters as sex education and condom distribution.* The approaches discussed have proven to be effective in curbing HIV/AIDS, but are offensive to large numbers of people in many of the worst-affected countries.

In both cases, progress will depend on political commitment and the involvement of multiple stakeholders to arrive at sustainable solutions, both from resource and consensual points of view. Comprehensive approaches will need to be developed, involving parents, schools, religious institutions, and the private sector. Research can play an important role in helping policymakers and stakeholders come to grips with the complex links between HIV/AIDS and education. A rich payoff may be expected, for example, from research on the epidemic's impact on economic growth and teacher attrition rates, the consequences of orphanhood for school achievement and economic growth, and the impact of school-based interventions.

5

The World Bank's Role

The World Bank has been a long-standing partner to developing countries in their efforts to educate their people, and to date is the largest external source of financing for education and for HIV/AIDS programs and activities worldwide. It has, equally, been at the forefront of efforts to put HIV/AIDS on the global development agenda. The Bank is deeply committed to supporting the world in an education-centered fight against AIDS—an objective that resonates strongly with its mission of poverty reduction. This objective also fits squarely within the Bank's strategic framework, which emphasizes support to countries to invest in people and to strengthen the investment climate as the basis for progress toward the Millennium Development Goals.

The Bank is well positioned to help countries open the window of hope that education offers by virtue of its dialogue with most of the world's developing countries and its current commitment of US$23.7 billion to 397 active projects in the human development sectors worldwide. In terms of the advocacy role for which the Bank is especially well equipped, key priorities relevant to education are to (a) help strengthen political commitment for Education for All (EFA) and anti-AIDS efforts; (b) build awareness at high, as well as functional, levels of government of the importance of education in the fight against HIV/AIDS; and (c) support macroeconomic reforms—with careful attention to their social implications—to ensure the needed national context for the achievement of education goals.

As relevant as the Bank's global reach are its partnerships with key global partners and its financial support to countries, not only the poorest countries receiving concessional finance, but also middle-income countries that otherwise have limited access to long-term capital of the kind needed for investment in human development. The Bank can also offer its clients the benefit of its broad diagnostic capabilities and operational experience by sharing best practices and lessons learned, particularly in the area of social sectors and social funds.

The Bank's work in education is centered on two priorities. The first is EFA, which includes the objectives of universal primary education and gender equity in schooling. Support for EFA accounts for a significant part of the Bank's ongoing activities. Second, the Bank's strategy for education recognizes that EFA is not so much an end in itself, as a first step along the continuum of lifelong learning for children to maximize their potential as individuals and as members of a productive society. A growing area of support will therefore be education for the knowledge economy, which is crucial to the broader development of skills and competencies that will strengthen national competitiveness in the global arena, and are thus fundamental to economic well-being and poverty reduction.

An urgent challenge is to integrate HIV/AIDS issues into the Bank's dual-focused support. A call for such action has most recently been voiced by the Group of Eight Task Force on Education, established in 2001 to accelerate progress on EFA. For the Bank, this directive implies helping countries to (a) pursue overall education goals more vigorously while factoring in the epidemic's impact; and (b) ensure adequate education aimed specifically at HIV/AIDS prevention. As with all Bank assistance, such support would entail first, helping build consensus around these priorities within a country and across its external partners. Notably, countries would drive this process as part of preparing nationally owned development strategies (Poverty Reduction Strategy Papers [PRSPs] in the case of low-income countries). Second, such support would also entail assistance for implementing these strategies, once agreed on, through lending and nonlending services, including analytical and advisory services, knowledge-sharing services, and technical assistance, on the basis of country demand and comparative advantage across external partners.

As noted earlier, EFA support is gaining momentum. In support of the work of the Group of Eight Task Force, the Bank has undertaken a country-by-country analysis of financing requirements for achieving EFA and the preparation of a paper synthesizing policy options for EFA achievement. The analysis rests on a broad framework of national policies, envisaged by the Bank, for attaining EFA (box 5-1). Wherever relevant, the projections for EFA attainment and financing requirements factor in the impact of HIV/AIDS, drawing on the Education and HIV/AIDS (Ed-SIDA/AIDS) model. "With" and "without AIDS" comparisons (see the examples presented in figure 5-1) are vital in helping countries to appreciate the dimensions of the problem they face and develop the commensurate commitment to act with urgency, design effective responses, and mobilize the needed financial and human resources. Currently analyses suggest that HIV/AIDS is likely to increase the annual demand for external support to achieve EFA in the range of US$450 million to US$550 million.

Box 5-1. EFA: What will it take?

- *Strong government commitment.* Ensure a sound macroeconomic climate, adequate tax effort and resource mobilization, and adequate spending on primary education.
- *Focus on access and quality of learning.* Bring out-of-school children into school and ensure adequate teacher salaries, training, and other inputs to keep children in school.
- *Education system efficiency.* Limit primary cycle repetition, set a ceiling on teachers' salaries, and contain classroom construction costs.
- *Special focus.* Emphasize girls' education, Africa and South Asia, impact of HIV/AIDS, impact of conflict.

Figure 5-1. Primary school net enrollment ratio in presence and absence of HIV/AIDS, 1990–2014

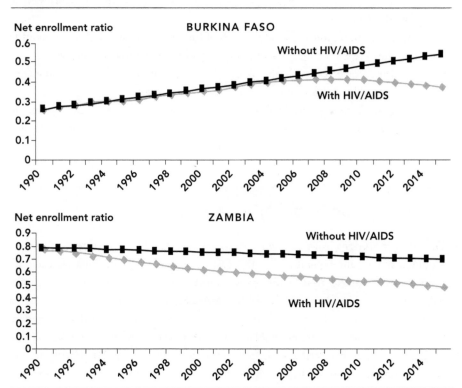

Note: These figures extrapolate the future based on historical trends. The impact of HIV/AIDS is calculated using teacher-student ratios projected from the output of country-specific Ed-SIDA/AIDS models developed by education planners from each of these countries.

Source: http://sima.mdg.

Prioritized attention to girls' education, the Africa and South Asia regions, and countries in conflict will not only improve progress on EFA, but will also benefit the HIV/AIDS agenda, as each of these areas are foci of vulnerability. Support for girls' education is already a priority for the Bank: over the last five years new commitments for girls' education projects have averaged nearly 60 percent of total primary and secondary education lending. The Bank is helping countries pursue a variety of strategies to keep girls in school, including the provision of scholarships, free textbooks, sanitation facilities, HIV/AIDS instruction, gender sensitivity training, and safe transport to and from school. While instability and limited absorptive capacity have constrained the growth of lending volumes to Africa, the Bank is actively engaged in the region to provide support wherever circumstances promise the effective use of resources.

The following broad principles that underlie all Bank support for education are discussed further in subsequent sections. Each entails significant collaboration with strategic partners.

- Scaling up successful approaches, given the enormity of the EFA, as well as HIV/AIDS, challenges
- Promoting innovation as a crucial means of finding timely and flexible solutions to unraveling crisis situations that lack a history of tried and tested responses
- Mobilizing resources, with the Bank playing a catalytic role and encouraging domestic public and private investment as much as possible
- Contributing to capacity building and knowledge-generation and -sharing to strengthen countries' information and analytical base so they can better define their own problems and develop solutions with the benefit of global best-practice.

Scaling up successful approaches

The Bank is working with partners to make some effective approaches available to education systems throughout Africa. In a first phase of activity, the Bank worked with partners in 10 countries to help education planners develop a response to the impact of HIV/AIDS on education, using the Ed-SIDA/AIDS planning tool (see box 5-2 for an example from Nigeria). Training in this approach will now be made available throughout Africa to countries developing Bank-supported education projects. The Bank has similarly worked in partnership to help countries implement HIV/AIDS prevention in schools, using the Focusing Resources of Effective School Health (FRESH) framework approach developed by a consortium of agencies. The FRESH approach is part of more than 20 projects in Africa, and efforts are now being intensified to assist all countries in Africa to incorporate this approach into education systems supported by Bank projects.

Box 5-2. Protecting Nigeria's education systems: Planning is indispensable

Nigeria is in the early stages of the HIV/AIDS epidemic. The median prevalence of HIV infection is 5 percent, but in some states is now approaching 20 percent. Nearly a fourth of Africa's schoolchildren live in Nigeria. Thus proactive efforts to safeguard the country's education systems can yield enormous future benefits. Failure to anticipate the epidemic's impact, however, all but assures national decline.

The government recognizes the urgent need for action, guided by an informed planning process. In March 2001 the ministry of education turned to the Ed-SIDA/AIDS planning tool developed by the World Bank and other partners to help countries assess the impact of HIV/AIDS. Preliminary projections from a workshop funded jointly by the Department for International Development (United Kingdom) and the Bank, and with support from the United Nations Educational, Scientific, and Cultural Organization and the International Institute for Educational Planning, pointed to a sharp drop in teacher numbers coupled with a 35 percent increase in the school-age population. The government moved quickly to train the country's education planners, beginning with the five most populous states. This approach is helping planners assess the localized impact of the epidemic and design responses accordingly.

Promoting innovation

The Bank recognizes the need for innovative and flexible approaches, especially for the worst-affected countries and the most vulnerable groups, such as orphans and youth. Efforts in this vein have included support for (a) *Heart and Soul,* a Kenyan soap opera that promises to bring "edutainment" themes of reducing promiscuity and promoting human rights to wide audiences beginning in early 2002; (b) the Hope for African Children Initiative, which aims to build awareness and ensure the health and education of Africa's orphans; and (c) innovative approaches for dealing with out-of-school children and youth, including a pilot Philippine project that has helped provide learning opportunities to 6- to 24-year-olds, prepare high school dropouts for employment, build institutional capacity to address such needs, and involve businesses in the effort.

Mobilizing resources

Strengthening the Bank's advocacy role will be crucial to reinforcing political commitment for EFA, both as an end in itself and as an important weapon in fighting AIDS. An important objective of advocacy is to help close the financing gap for meeting EFA goals, which is already large for some countries and further widened as a result of the epidemic. There is a need to increase both the overall level of external support and the share allocated to education.

Globally, 143 Bank-financed education projects were under implementation in 78 countries as of December 2001, reflecting investments of US$9.7 billion. The Bank aims to support countries in modifying existing projects along the lines described in table 4-2 and in ensuring that new EFA and girls' education projects include a specific response to HIV/AIDS wherever relevant. Health and social sector protection projects may also be multisectoral and benefit education, and there is a specific aim to expand the share of support for orphans and vulnerable children.

The granting of debt relief under the Heavily Indebted Poor Countries (HIPC) Initiative constitutes a landmark effort, undertaken jointly with the International Monetary Fund, to mobilize global resources for some of the world's poorest countries. One prerequisite for HIPC debt relief is the preparation of PRSPs to govern the use of freed up public resources, channeling them toward increased social spending, including for pursuit of EFA and for HIV/AIDS prevention. To date, a total of US$36 billion in debt savings has been committed to 24 countries. As a result, social spending in these countries is projected to increase by some US$2.2 billion per year over the next three years, and early indications are that some 40 percent of HIPC relief will be directed to education and 25 percent to health. A vital task is therefore to ensure that PRSPs address a country's education sector needs, factoring in the impact of HIV/AIDS.

In addition, the multisectoral Multicountry HIV/AIDS Program (MAP) for Africa has committed US$462.5 million to 12 countries (see box 5-3 for the example of Uganda), and a similar initiative has made US$53.5 million available to Caribbean countries. A multisectoral response—including the education sector—is a central strategy for all these MAP projects, and in the US$500 million second phase (MAP II) the role of the education sector is specifically emphasized.

Generating and sharing knowledge

Given its global presence and commitment to learning lessons and sharing knowledge, the Bank can play a major role in helping countries draw on worldwide and regional best practice and undertake analytical work to ensure sound approaches and effective use of

Box 5-3. Uganda HIV/AIDS Control Project: A best-practice role for education

One of 12 credits approved by the Bank thus far under the MAP for Africa, on concessional International Development Association terms, was the Uganda HIV/AIDS Control Project. The project will finance a US$50 million share of Uganda's HIV/AIDS program, focusing on prevention and the scaling up of efforts by mainstreaming program activities into line ministries. Under the program, the ministry of education will

- Review education sector policies regarding access to school by children and teachers with HIV/AIDS, sanctions against sexual harassment, and sexual abuse by teachers and others.
- Review primary, secondary, and tertiary curricula to include appropriate reproductive health and HIV-related education, produce relevant education materials, and train teachers in the use of these materials.
- Focus resources on effective school health (the FRESH approach). Lessons will expand HIV-related knowledge and seek behavioral change through a teaching approach to include negotiation, resistance to peer pressure, self-esteem, communication, and assertion. Teacher training colleges will develop lessons.
- Promote initiatives led by school and student associations (all levels).
- Expand HIV/AIDS and sexually transmitted infection–counseling and testing to schools, colleges, and institutions of higher education using peers and parents as key resources.
- Monitor and evaluate the impact of HIV/AIDS on the education sector, in collaboration with other ministries and agencies.
- Provide HIV/AIDS-related information, education, and communication, and distribute condoms to ministry work forces.

resources. Continuous learning from the first phase of the Bank-supported MAP projects in Africa will be an urgent priority to improve the quality of existing projects and to inform the design of the second phase projects. The impact of key approaches in education programs needs to be evaluated across several countries. This paper presents some promising approaches, but the education systems of countries facing the epidemic require more specific information on the relative cost-effectiveness of these approaches.

Expanding and consolidating Web-based "gateways" is another priority. For example, vehicles such as the FRESH Web site or the Development Education Program of the World Bank Institute—the Bank's learning arm—are already serving users interested in innovations in school health, HIV prevention, and other cross-cutting information relevant to schools. The Bank is also working with partners to develop an HIV/AIDS

Prevention Sourcebook that brings together best practice on school-based prevention methods. Other analytical work has sought to strengthen knowledge in specific areas (box 5-4) and to underpin Bank strategy, for example, in distance education, tertiary education, and science and technology. Urgent priorities for forthcoming analysis include assessing the impact of sectoral responses to the AIDS epidemic and finding solutions to the challenge of the vastly increasing numbers of orphans and other vulnerable children.

Box 5-4. Advocating behavioral change in Thailand

Thailand's Response to AIDS: Building on Success, Confronting the Future is a World Bank-commissioned report that summarizes recommendations derived from consultations in June 2000 with government officials, international agencies, nongovernmental organizations (NGOs), and research institutes about their perspectives on the Thai HIV/AIDS control program.

While Thailand's success in fighting AIDS is world-renowned, the report warns against complacency. One concern—of many—is the increase of infection among children. A decade ago, virtually all infections were among adults, more than 80 percent of them linked to commercial sex; however, a projection for 2000 estimated that 4,000 out of 29,000 new infections would be among children.

The report further flags the changing patterns of risk behavior among Thailand's young adults, noting their reduced indulgence in commercial sex, but greater engagement in other types of relationships—combined with low condom use—that expose them to high risk. The report calls for

- Intensifying and expanding behavior change education and training for HIV prevention among youth
- Promoting peer education, sex and reproductive health education, and life skills training to youth and young adults in school and workplace settings
- Tailoring messages to the new patterns of behavior and emphasizing condom use
- Forging partnerships between ministries, NGOs, community organizations, and the business sector in assuring adequate resources and coverage of programs to reduce risk among youth.

Building capacity

The need for capacity building is enormous, as the countries most challenged by EFA and HIV/AIDS objectives are in many cases the ones least equipped to attract resources, use them effectively, and demonstrate their effective use. Bank support will cover three important areas. First, the Bank will help ministries of education make the case—to national leaders, finance ministers, and the public—for high priority for the sector, not just for an increased share of resources for education, but an increase in the overall level of support commensurate with the sector's importance. Helping a country's education sector collaborate across sectors and establish its place in national HIV/AIDS efforts is a related priority. Second, the Bank is expanding its work with partners to provide training in the use of education planning tools, such as the Ed-SIDA/AIDS model. Third is support for building education sector capacity to collect data and analyze education statistics, an endeavor whose importance cannot be overstated.

Working with strategic partners

Partnership is crucial for the success of all these endeavors. EFA, the Millennium Development Goals, and progress on bridging the digital divide through knowledge economies are all universally endorsed objectives that require the coming together of many actors within and across countries. In its development work in general, and in the education sector in particular, the Bank has increasingly sought to work with strategic partners with the objective of scaling up results, mobilizing resources, making the best use of comparative advantage and experience, and building consensus. Examples of results-driven collaboration in the education and prevention spheres include FRESH and the Ed-SIDA/AIDS model, as well as important partnerships in the fight against AIDS (Box 5-5). On EFA, the Bank is taking the lead in working with various partners to analyze the policy and resource gaps for meeting the goals. Analysis will cover donor funding for basic education, the impact of debt relief on education expenditures, and the integration of national EFA plans into countries' PRSPs.

Box 5-5. Partnering to prevent youth infection

The Bank is a member of the U.N. Interagency Working Group on schools and education, a partnership that facilitates countries' development of strategic plans for HIV/AIDS prevention and impact management in education systems. The group's work focuses on the global HIV target of achieving a 25 percent reduction in infection rates among young people in the worst-affected countries by 2005 and globally by 2010.

Efforts aim to help countries manage the epidemic's impact on education systems and improve their capacity to reduce vulnerability to HIV/AIDS and to implement full-scale prevention programs, particularly in schools. Key outcomes are for all schools to match teacher supply and demand and to provide high-quality, skills-based prevention programs, and for all children and youth to receive good quality education.

Appendix: Prospects for Achieving EFA Goals

Country	Countries at risk on primary completion	Countries at risk on primary enrollment	Countries at risk on gender disparity in primary completion or enrollment	Countries with >2% HIV prevalence or large numbers of infected people [a]	Countries in or recovering from conflict	Countries not at risk on primary enrollment or completion
IDA countries (including blend): IDA & IBRD countries						
Afghanistan	X	X	X		X	
Albania	X		X			
Angola	X	X	X	X	X	
Armenia	X		X			
Azerbaijan						X
Bangladesh						X
Benin	X		X	X		
Bhutan	X		X			
Bolivia	X					
Bosnia and Herzegovina	X					
Burkina Faso	X	X	X	XX		
Burundi	X	X	X	XXX	X	
Cambodia	X		X	X	X	
Cameroon	X	X	X	XX		
Cape Verde						X
Central African Republic	X	X	X	XXX		
Chad	X	X	X	X	X	
Comoros	X	X	X			
Congo, Democratic Republic of	X	X	X	XX	X	
Congo, Republic of	X	X	X	XX		
Côte d'Ivoire	X	X	X	XXX		
Djibouti	X	X	X	XXX		
Dominica						X

Country	Countries at risk on primary completion	Countries at risk on primary enrollment	Countries at risk on gender disparity in primary completion or enrollment	Countries with >2% HIV prevalence or large numbers of infected people [a]	Countries in or recovering from conflict	Countries not at risk on primary enrollment or completion
Eritrea	X	X	X	X	X	
Ethiopia	X	X	X	XXX	X	
Gambia, The			X	X		X
Georgia	X					
Ghana	X	X	X	X		
Grenada						X
Guinea	X		X			
Guinea-Bissau	X		X	X		
Guyana	X			X		
Haiti				XX	X	X
Honduras	X					
India	X	X	X	X		
Indonesia	X					
Kenya	X	X		XXX		
Kiribati	X					
Kyrgyz Republic						X
Lao, People's Democratic Republic			X			X
Lesotho	X		X	XXX		
Liberia	X		X	X	X	
Madagascar	X					
Malawi			X	XXX		X
Maldives						X
Mali	X		X	X		
Mauritania	X		X			
Moldova						X
Mongolia	X		X			
Mozambique	X	X	X	XXX	X	
Myanmar	X			X		
Nepal	X		X		X	
Nicaragua						X
Niger	X	X	X			
Nigeria	X	X	X	X		
Pakistan	X		X			
Rwanda	X			XXX	X	
Samoa						X
São Tomé and Principe	X					
Senegal	X	X	X	X		
Sierra Leone	X	X	X	XXX	X	
Solomon Islands	X		X			
Somalia	X	X	X		X	

Country	Countries at risk on primary completion	Countries at risk on primary enrollment	Countries at risk on gender disparity in primary completion or enrollment	Countries with >2% HIV prevalence or large numbers of infected people [a]	Countries in or recovering from conflict	Countries not at risk on primary enrollment or completion
Sri Lanka					X	X
St. Lucia						X
St. Vincent and the Grenadines						X
Sudan	X	X	X		X	
Tajikistan						X
Tanzania	X	X		XX		
Togo			X	XX		X
Tonga						X
Uganda	X		X	XX		
Uzbekistan		X				X
Vanuatu	X		X			
Vietnam						X
Yemen, Republic of	X	X	X			
Yugoslavia, Federal Republic of		X				X
Zambia	X		X	XXX		
Zimbabwe				XXX		X
IDA subtotal	**55**	**28**	**46**	**36**	**17**	**24**
IBRD Countries						
Algeria						X
Antigua and Barbuda						X
Argentina						X
Bahamas, The [b]				X		X
Bahrain [b]	X		X			
Belarus	X					
Belize	X					
Botswana			X	XXX		X
Brazil				X		X
Bulgaria						X
Chile	X					
China						X
Colombia						X
Costa Rica						X
Croatia	X					
Czech Republic						X
Cuba [b]						X
Dominican Republic	X			XXX		
East Timor [b]	X				X	
Ecuador						X
Egypt, Arab Republic of			X			X

Country	Countries at risk on primary completion	Countries at risk on primary enrollment	Countries at risk on gender disparity in primary completion or enrollment	Countries with >2% HIV prevalence or large numbers of infected people [a]	Countries in or recovering from conflict	Countries not at risk on primary enrollment or completion
El Salvador						X
Equatorial Guinea	X					
Estonia	X					
Fiji						X
Gabon				X		X
Guatemala	X		X			
Hungary						X
Iran, Islamic Republic of	X		X			
Iraq	X		X		X	
Jamaica	X					
Jordan	X	X				
Kazakhstan						X
Korean, Dem. People's Rep. of[b]	X					
Korea, Republic of						X
Kuwait [b]						X
Latvia						X
Lebanon	X					
Lithuania						X
Macedonia, former Yugoslav Rep. of						X
Malaysia	X					
Marshall Islands						X
Mauritius						X
Mexico	X					
Micronesia, Federated States of	X					
Morocco	X		X			
Namibia				XXX		X
Oman [b]						X
Papua New Guinea	X	X	X			
Palau						X
Panama	X					
Paraguay						X
Peru						X
Philippines						X
Poland						X
Qatar [b]	X					
Romania						X
Russian Federation	X					
St. Kitts and Nevis	X					
Seychelles						X
Slovak Republic						X

Country	Countries at risk on primary completion	Countries at risk on primary enrollment	Countries at risk on gender disparity in primary completion or enrollment	Countries with >2% HIV prevalence or large numbers of infected people [a]	Countries in or recovering from conflict	Countries not at risk on primary enrollment or completion
Slovenia	X					
South Africa			X	XXX		X
Suriname						X
Swaziland			X	XXX		X
Syrian Arab Republic	X					
Thailand	X			X		
Trinidad and Tobago	X					
Tunisia						X
Turkey			X			X
Turkmenistan	X					
Ukraine	X	X				
United Arab Republic	X					
Uruguay						X
Venezuela, República Bolivariana de	X	X				
West Bank and Gaza [b]						X
IBRD subtotal	**33**	**4**	**11**	**9**	**1**	**43**
IDA + IBRD total	**88**	**32**	**57**	**45**	**18**	**67**

Summary:		Total countries	Countries at risk on primary completion
	IDA	79	55
	IBRD (including non-borrowers)	76	33
		155	**88**

IBRD: International Bank for Reconstruction and Development.
IDA: International Development Association.

[a.] XX indicates countries with HIV prevalence greater than 5 percent and XXX indicates countries with HIV prevalance greater than 10 percent.

[b.] These countries are not IBRD borrowers.

Note: This table may be adjusted to reflect finalization of EFA country analysis currently under way.

Bibliography

African Development Forum. 2000. "The Leadership Challenge and the Way Forward: HIV/AIDS and Education in Eastern and Southern Africa." Paper presented at the African Development Forum 2000, Addis Ababa, Ethiopia. Available at http://www.uneca.org/adf2000/educ0.htm.

Ainsworth, M., and D. Filmer. Forthcoming. *Poverty, AIDS, and Children's Welfare: A Targeting Dilemma.*

Ainsworth, M., and W. Teokul. 2000. "Breaking the Silence: Setting Realistic Priorities for AIDS Control in Less-Developed Countries. *Lancet* 356 (2993): 55–60.

Ainsworth, M., K. Beegle, and G. Koda. 2001. "The Impact of Adult Mortality on Primary School Enrollment in Northwestern Tanzania." Background paper for the Africa Development Forum 2000, Addis Ababa, Ethiopia. UNAIDS, Geneva.

Badcock-Walters, P. 2001. "The Impact of HIV/AIDS on Education in KwaZulu Natal." KZNDEC Provincial Education Development Unit, Durban, South Africa.

Bakaki, P. 2001. "The Orphan Study Activity in Uganda." A report submitted to the Nutrition and Early Childhood Development Project. Ministry of Health, Kampala, Uganda.

Barnet, E., K. de Koning, and V. Francis. 1995. "Health and HIV/AIDS Education in Primary and Secondary Schools in Africa and Asia." Education Research no. 14. Overseas Development Administration, London.

Bennel, P. 2000. "Improving Youth Livelihoods in Sub-Saharan Africa. A Review of Policies and Programmes with Particular Reference to the Link between Sexual Behaviour and Economic Well-Being." USAID, Washington, D.C.

Bonnel, René. 2001. *Cost of Scaling HIV Program Activities to a National Level in Sub-Saharan Africa: Methods and Estimates.* Washington, D.C.: World Bank, ACTAfrica.

Caceres, C. F., A. M. Rosasco, J. S. Mandel, and N. Hearst. 1994. "Evaluating a School-Based Intervention for STD/AIDS Prevention in Peru." *Journal of Adolescent Health* 15: 582–91.

Caldwell, B., I. Pieris, B. Khuda, J. Caldwell, and P. Caldwell. 1999. "Sexual Regimes and Sexual Networking: The Risk of an HIV/AIDS Epidemic in Bangladesh." *Social Science & Medicine* 48: 1103–16.

Chipfakacha, V. G. 1997. "STD/HIV/AIDS Knowledge, Beliefs, and Practices of Traditional Healers in Botswana." *AIDS Care* 4: 417–25.

Christian Aid. 2001. "No Excuses. Facing up to Sub-Saharan Africa's AIDS Orphans Crisis." Available at: http://www.christian-aid.org.uk/indepth/0105aids/aidsorph.htm.

Connolly, M. 2001. "Principles to Guide Programming for Orphans and Other Vulnerable Children." Draft. UNICEF, Child Protection Section, New York.

Coombe, C. 2000a. "Keeping the Education System Healthy: Managing the Impact of HIV/AIDS on Education in South Africa." *Current Issues in Comparative Education* 3(1). Available at: www.tc.columbia.edu/cice/vol03nr1/ccart1.htm.

———. 2000b. "Managing the Impact of HIV/AIDS on the Education Sector." University of Pretoria, Centre for the Study of AIDS, Pretoria, South Africa. Available at: www.csa.za.org/filemanager/list/6.

———. 2001. "Rethinking some of Our Perceptions about HIV/AIDS and Education." Paper prepared for the Southern African Development Community (SADC) meeting on HIV/AIDS and Education. February 26–28, University of Pretoria, Pretoria, South Africa.

Coombe, C., and M. Kelly. 2001. "Education as a Vehicle for Combating HIV/AIDS." *UNESCO Prospects* XXXI(3): 435–45.

Deininger, K., M. Garcia, and K. Subbarao. 2001. "AIDS-Induced Orphanhood as a Systemic Shock: Magnitude, Impact, and Program Interventions in Africa." Paper presented at the International Conference on Crises and Disasters: Measurement and Mitigation of their Human Costs, organized by the International Food Policy Research Institute, and the Inter-American Development Bank, November 13–14, Washington, D.C.

Department for International Development, United Kingdom. 2001. "HIV/AIDS Strategy." London.

Education Development Center, Inc. 2000a. "Final Report, Global Forum on the Impact of HIV/AIDS on Education Systems: Focus on Africa." Lusaka, Zambia

————.2000b. "Interactive Radio in Zambia for Out-of-School Audiences: October 2000 Evaluation." U.S. Agency for International Development, Zambia.

Family Health International. 1996. "HIV/AIDS Peer Education: Evolving with the Epidemic." *AIDScaptions* III(3).

Fawole, I. O., M. C. Asuzu, S. O. Oduntan, and W. R. Brieger. 1999. "A School-Based AIDS Education Programme for Secondary School Students in Nigeria: A Review of Effectiveness." *Health Education Research—Theory & Practice* 14: 675–83.

Foster, G., and J. Williamson. 2001. "A Review of Current Literature on the Impact of HIV/AIDS on Children in Sub-Saharan Africa." *AIDS 2000* 14(suppl 3): S275–S284.

Gachuhi, D. 1999. "The Impact of HIV/AIDS on Education Systems in the Eastern and Southern Africa Region and the Response of Education Systems to HIV/AIDS: Life Skills Programs." Paper prepared for UNICEF presentation at the Sub-Saharan Africa Conference on EFA 2000, December 6–10, 1999, Johannesburg, South Africa.

Garnett, G. P., N. C. Grassly, and S. Gregson S. 2001. "AIDS: The Makings of a development Disaster?" *Journal of International Development* 13: 391–409.

Gatawa, B. G. 1995. "Zimbabwe: AIDS Education for Schools." UNICEF. Harare, Zimbabwe.

Gold, M. R., J. E. Siegel, L. B. Russell, and M. C. Weinstein, eds. 1996. *Cost-Effectiveness in Health and Medicine.* New York: Oxford University Press.

Government of Botswana and DfID. 2000. "The Impact on HIV/AIDS of Primary and Secondary Education in Botswana: Developing a Comprehensive Strategic Response." DfID, London.

Gregson, S., H. Waddell, and S. Chandiwana. 2001. "School Education and HIV Control in Sub-Saharan Africa: From Discord to Harmony? *Journal of International Development* 13: 467–85.

Harris, A. M., and J. G. Schubert. 2001. "Defining 'Quality' in the Midst of HIV/AIDS: Ripple Effects in the Classroom. IEQ Project." Paper presented at the 44th annual meeting of the Comparative Education Society, March, Washington, D.C.

Helland, A.-M., J. Lexow, and E. Carm. 1999. "The Impact of HIV/AIDS on Education." LINS Report 1999-4. Norwegian Agency for Development Cooperation. Oslo, Norway

Hepburn, H. 2001. "Primary Education in Eastern and Southern Africa: Increasing Access for Orphans and Vulnerable Children in AIDS-Affected Areas. Displaced Children and Orphans Fund. Available on:
http://www.usaid.gov/pop_health/dcofwvf/reports/hepburn.html.

Herbison, F., and M. Charles, eds. 1965. *Manpower and Education.* New York: McGraw-Hill.

Hubley, J. 2000. "Interventions Targeted at Youth Aimed at Influencing Sexual Behavior and AIDS/STDs." Leeds Health Education Database, April 2000. Leeds, United Kingdom

Hunter, S., and J. Williamson. 1997. "Children on the Brink: Strategies to Support Children Isolated by HIV/AIDS." U.S. Agency for International Development. Washington, D.C.

———. 2000. "Children on the Brink 2000: Updated Estimates and Recommendations for Intervention." U.S. Agency for International Development. Washington, D.C.

Kelly, M. J. 1999. "The Impact of HIV/AIDS on Schooling in Zambia." Paper presented at the XIth International Conference on AIDS and STDs in Africa, Lusaka, Zambia.

———. 2000a. "Planning for Education in the Context of HIV/AIDS." UNESCO, International Institute for Educational Planning. Paris, France.

———. 2000b. "Standing Education on Its Head: Aspects of Schooling in a World with HIV/AIDS." *Current Issues in Comparative Education* 3(1). Available at: www.tc.columbia.edu/cice/ vol03nr1/mkart1.htm.

———. 2000c. *The Encounter between HIV/AIDS and Education.* Harare, Zimbabwe: UNESCO, Sub-Regional Office for Southern Africa.

———. 2000d. "HIV/AIDS and Education in Eastern and Southern Africa. The Leadership Challenge and the Way Forward." Report for the African Development Forum.

———. 2001. *Challenging the Challenger: Understanding and Expanding the Response of Universities in Africa to HIV/AIDS.* ADEA and World Bank. A Synthesis Report for the Working Group on Higher Education (WGHE), Association for the Development of Education in Africa (ADEA). Washington, D.C.: World Bank.

Kinsman, J., S. Harrison, E. J. Kengeya-Kayondo, S. Musoke, and J. Whitworth. 1999. "Implementation of a Comprehensive AIDS Education Programme for Schools in Masaka District, Uganda." *AIDS Care* 11(5): 591–601.

Kirby, D., L. Short, J. Collins, D. Rugg, L. Kolbe, M. Howard, B. Miller, F. Sonenstein, and L. S. Zabib. 1994. "School-Based Programs to Reduce Risk Behaviors: A Review of Effectiveness." *Public Health Reports* 109: 339–61.

Krueger, A., and L. Mikael. 2000. "Education for Growth: Why and for Whom?" Working Paper Series. National Bureau of Economic Research, Cambridge, Massachusetts.

Lloyd-Rowe, A., and R. Ballard. 2000. "National Training." Paper presented at the conference on Life Skills in HIV/AIDS Education, August 14–25, Conakary, Guinea, UNICEF and World Bank.

Malambo, R. M. 2000. "The Views of Teachers and Pupils on the Teaching of HIV/AIDS in Basic Education: A Case Study of Zambia's Southern and Lusaka Provinces. *Current Issues in Comparative Education* 3(1). Available at: www.tc.columbia.edu/cice/vol03nr1/rmart1.htm.

Milimo, J. T. 1998. "Factors Affecting School Attendance. A Qualitative Approach." Ministry of Education, Participatory Assessment Group for Study Fund Investigation of Factors Affecting School Attendance, Lusaka, Zambia.

Ministry of Education. 2001. "HIV/AIDS Strategic Plan. Third Draft of Vision, Goals, and Objectives." Siavonga, Zambia.

Morgan, D, and J. A. G. Whitworth. 2001. "The Natural History of HIV-1 Infection in Africa. *Nature Medicine* 7: 143–45.

Multi-Country Report on the Ed-SIDA Initiative, Part IIA. 2001. "Analysis of Interventions in the Fight against AIDS at the School Level." Paper presented at the Senior Experts Conference on HIV/AIDS and Education, March, El Mina, Ghana.

———. 2001. "I: Estimating the Importance of HIV/AIDS for the Education Systems of West Africa: A Tool for Educational Planners." Paper presented at the Senior Experts Conference on HIV/AIDS and Education in the West African Economic Community Countries, March, Accra, Ghana.

Mwikisa, C. N., and G. Lungwangwa. 1998. "Education Indicators, Costs, and Factors Associated with Primary School Effectiveness in Zambia." Ministry of Education, Lusaka, Zambia.

Nampanya-Serpell, N. 2000. "Social and Economic Risk Factors for HIV/AIDS-Affected Families in Zambia." Paper presented at the AIDS and Economics Symposium, July 7–8, Durban, South Africa.

Ndlovu, R., and B. Kaim. 1999. "Adolescent Reproductive Health Education Project: Lessons From 'Auntie Stella': Reproductive Health Education in Zimbabwe's Secondary Schools. Part One." Report. A Report by the Adolescent Reproductive Health Education Project on behalf of the Zimbabwe Ministry of Education, Sport and Culture and the Training and Research Support Centre. Harare.

Odaga, A., and W. Heneveld. 1995. *Girls and Schools in Sub-Saharan Africa: From Analysis to Action.* Technical Paper no. 298. Africa Technical Department Series. Washington, D.C.: World Bank.

Over, M. 1998. "The Effects of Societal Variable on Urban Rates of HIV Infection in Developing Countries: An Exploratory Analysis." In Martha Ainsworth, Lieve Fransen, and Mead Over, eds., *Confronting AIDS: Evidence from the Developing World.* Brussels and Washington, D.C.: European Commission and World Bank.

Partnership for Child Development. 1998. "Implications for School-Based Health Programs of Age and Gender Patterns in the Tanzanian Primary School. *Tropical Medicine and International Health* 3(10): 850–53.

Perraton, H. 1997. "The Cost-Effectiveness of Distance Education for Primary Teacher Training." Report prepared for the International Research Foundation for Open Learning for the Commonwealth of Learning and the Asian Development Bank. Available at: http://www.col.org/irfol/.

Population Council. 2000. "Peer Education and HIV/AIDS: Past Experience, Future Directions." UNAIDS and Horizons. Washington, D.C.

Seifert, K. 1997. *Early Intervention: HIV/AIDS Programs for School-Aged Youth.* Office of Sustainable Development, Bureau for Africa. Washington, D.C.: U.S. Agency for International Development.

Shaeffer, S. 1994. "The Impact of HIV/AIDS on Education: A Review of Literature and Experience." UNESCO. Paris.

Shuey, D. A., B. B. Babishangire, S. Omiat, and H. Bagarukayo. 1999. "Increased Sexual Abstinence among In-School Adolescents as a Result of School Health Education in Soroti District, Uganda." *Health Education Research* 14(3): 411–19.

Siamwiza, R. 1998. "A Situation Analysis of Policy and Teaching HIV/AIDS Prevention in Educational Institutions in Zambia. UNESCO/UNAIDS Project on Integrating HIV/AIDS Prevention in School Curricula." UNESCO and UNAIDS.

Soul City. 2000. "Soul City 4 Impact Evaluation: AIDS." Lusaka.

Stewart, H., A. McCauley, S. Baker, et al. 2001. "Reducing HIV Infection among Youth: What Can Schools Do? Key Baseline Findings from Mexico, South Africa, and Thailand." Horizons Program of the Population Council – ICRW, IMIFAP, MRC, PATH, Population Council.

Subbarao, K., A. Mattimore, and K. Plengemann. 2001. "Social Protection of Africa's Orphans and Other Vulnerable Children." Africa Region Human Development Working Paper Series. World Bank, Washington, D.C.

UNAIDS (United Nations Programme on HIV/AIDS). 1997a. "Integrating HIV/STD Prevention in the School Setting: A Position Paper." Geneva

———. 1997b. "Learning and Teaching about AIDS at School. UNAIDS technical update." UNAIDS Best-Practice Collection. Geneva

———. 1999a. "UNAIDS Best Practices: School AIDS Education Category. The Kenya Youth Initiatives Project." UNAIDS Best-Practice Collection. Geneva

———. 1999b. *Sexual Behavioral Change for HIV: Where Have all the Theories Taken Us?* Geneva.

———. 2000a. "Report on the Global HIV/AIDS Epidemic." Geneva.

———. 2000b. "AIDS Epidemic Update: December 2000." Geneva.

———. 2000c. "AIDS in Africa, Country by Country." UNAIDS and ECA. Geneva.

———. 2000d. *Innovative Approaches to HIV Prevention: Selected Case Studies.* Geneva.

———. 2000e. "Gender and HIV." Geneva.

———. 2000g. "AIDS and the Education Sector." Geneva.

———. 2000h. Collaboration with traditional healers in HIV/AIDS prevention and care in Sub-Saharan Africa: a literature review. Geneva.

———. 2001. "AIDS Epidemic Update: December 2001." Geneva.

UNAIDS (United Nations Programme on HIV/AIDS), UNICEF (United Nations Children's Fund), and National Black Leadership Commission on AIDs, Inc. (BLCA). 1999. "Call to Action for 'Children Left Behind' by AIDS." Washington, D.C.

UNESCO (United Nations Cultural, Scientific, and Cultural Organization). 2001a. "Strategic Resource Guide: Strategies for Action to Combat HIV/AIDS within the Education Sector." Ghana.

———. 2001b. *UNESCO's Strategy for HIV/AIDS Preventive Education.* Paris.

UNICEF (United Nations Children's Fund). 1998. "Impact du VIH/SIDA sur le systeme educatif Centrafricain." Bulletin no. 5. UNICEF, PNUD, and other partners. Bangui, Central African Republic.

UNICEF (United Nations Children's Fund), and UNAIDS (United Nations Programme on HIV/AIDS). 1999. *Children Orphaned by AIDS: Front-Line Responses from Eastern and Southern Africa.* New York and Washington D.C.

U.S. Agency for International Development. 2000. *Proceedings of a Colloquium on HIV/AIDS and Girls' Education.* Washington, D.C.: Office of Women in Development.

Vandemoortele, J., and E. Delamonica. 2000. "Education 'Vaccine' against HIV/AIDS." *Current Issues in Comparative Education* 3(1). Available at: www.tc.columbia.edu/cice/vol03nr1/jvedart1.htm.

Wang, L.Y., M. A. Davis, L. Robin, J. Collins, K. Coyle, and E. Baumler. 2000. "Economic Evaluation of Safer Choices: A School-Based Human Immunodeficiency Virus, Other Sexually Transmitted Diseases, and Pregnancy Prevention Program. *Archives of Pediatric and Adolescent Medicine,* 154: 1017–24.

World Bank. 1991. *Tanzania: AIDS Assessment and Planning Study.* A World Bank Country Study. Washington, D.C.

———. 1999. *Confronting AIDS: Public Priorities in a Global Epidemic.* A World Bank Policy Research Report. New York: Oxford University Press.

———. 2000a. "Education for All. From Jomtien to Dakar and Beyond." Paper prepared for the World Education Forum, April 26-28, Dakar, Senegal.

———. 2000b. *Intensifying Action against HIV/AIDS in Africa: Responding to a Development Crisis.* Washington, D.C.

———. 2001a. *Engendering Development: Through Gender Equality in Rights, Resources, and Voice.* World Bank Policy Research Report. New York: Oxford University Press.

———. 2001b. *Education for Dynamic Economies: Accelerating Progress towards Education for All.* Development Board Paper. Washington, D.C.

——— 2001c. *Education Poverty Reduction Strategy Paper Sourcebook.* Washington D.C.

———. 2001d. "Distance Education Strategy Paper for Africa." Africa Region, Human Development Group, Washington, D.C.

World Bank, ACTAfrica. 2000a. "Exploring the Implications of the HIV/AIDS Epidemic for Educational Planning in Selected African Countries: The Demographic Question." Washington, D.C.

———. 2000b. "Safeguarding Development in the Age of AIDS." Washington, D.C.

———. 2001a. "Costs of Scaling HIV Program Activities to a National Level in Sub-Saharan Africa: Methods and Estimates." Washington, D.C.

Useful URLs

UNAIDS:
www.unaids.org

UNICEF:
www.unicef.org

UNESCO:
www.unesco.org

World Bank:
www.worldbank.org

AIDS orphans assistance database:
http://orphans.fxb.org/db/index.html

Displaced Children's and Orphans' Fund:
http://www.usaid.gov/pop_health/dcofwvf/

School Health Data:
http://www.schoolsandhealth.org

World Health Organization:
http://www.who.int